THE
GARDENER'S
BOOK *of* DAYS

Facts, Fables and Folklore
from the World of Gardening

FAITH and GEOFFREY WHITEN

THE GARDENER'S BOOK OF DAYS

Faith and Geoffrey Whiten

First published in the United Kingdom by
The Edinburgh Publishing Company Limited,
Whittingehame, East Lothian, Scotland.

British Library Cataloguing in Publication Data
Whiten, Faith
Gardener's Book of Days, 1993
I. Title II. Whiten, Geoff
635
ISBN 1 874201 03 X

Cover illustration: The Pansy Garden, Munstead Wood, Surrey
by Thomas H. Hunn (1878-1908) by kind permission of the
Christopher Wood Gallery, London and The Bridgeman Art Library London.

Printed and bound in the United Kingdom by
Stephens & George Ltd, Merthyr Industrial Estate, Dowlais, Merthyr Tydfil, Mid Glamorgan, CF48 2TD

CONTENTS

FIRST CLASS - FIRST CHOICE

For many years the name Barlow Tyrie has been synonymous with high quality teak outdoor leisure furniture. Established in 1920, the family firm of Barlow Tyrie is now the United Kingdom's leading manufacturer of teak outdoor furniture, our designs are often the first choice of gardeners and garden designers. Perhaps it is a significant comment on our design integrity that our furniture is to be found at such august establishments as the British Museum, London, the Museum d'Orsay, Paris and the Barcelona Olympic Village, Spain. Our furniture is designed to complement an outdoor style of living whilst retaining a tasteful harmony with the natural surroundings.

DORSET DINING CHAIRS - STIRLING DINING TABLE

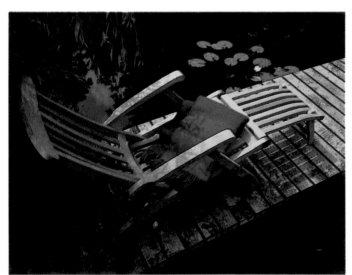

COMMODORE RECLINER

These classic designs have withstood the passage of time and fashion with distinction, remaining as popular today as when they were first introduced. New designs are only added to the range after much thought and deliberation, only the highest quality materials are used with traditional design details and construction methods being retained throughout. The range includes armchairs, seats, benches, dining tables, coffee tables, recliners, loungers, corner seats, a circular tree seat and a suite of folding furniture. Barlow Tyrie use only plantation grown Java teakwood and are listed in the *Good Wood Guide* published by the Friends of the Earth.

BARLOW TYRIE LIMITED
Teakwood outdoor Leisure Furniture
Braintrea, Essex CM7 7RN England. Tel: (0376) 322505 Fax: (0376) 347052

INTRODUCTION

Time is always important to gardeners. Time past, present and future. We look back and say to visitors, "Oh but you really should have seen the garden two weeks ago. The roses were a picture... " We look forward and resolve that a prize plant will do much better next year because of the weather, the fertilizer, the pruning... As for the present, that's always the right time to potter in the greenhouse or herbaceous border - time to pull just a few more weeds before it gets dark or it's time to cook dinner.

Even when we're not actually out in the garden, we like to think about what to do later. So, on dark winter evenings we sit indoors and pore over gardening books and seed catalogues; in warm sunshine we relax on the lawn with the gardening magazines. But all that advice, all those ideas add up to so much dreaming and scheming that it's quite wearing and potentially rather expensive.

Now *The Gardener's Book of Days* is different. It's aim is not to nag gardeners towards energetic endeavours, but to divert and entertain; to remind us that gardening is not only about being up and doing, but also about thinking, feeling, appreciating beauty or disagreeing with some opinionated fool.

We have dipped into a wealth of gardening literature, facts, figures, history and fable to evoke a whole range of emotions. Some offerings are light-hearted and amusing, others are sad and deeply moving. There are some wonderful lines by great poets and some tongue-in-cheek writing.

Historical insights are frequently into the ordinary, everyday endeavours of growers, gardeners and observers of the gardening scene. Where there is advice it may be useful, or may equally be so outrageous that nobody these days would think to follow it... or would they?

Visits to our local garden centre regularly remind us of the fact that in gardening there is always change - new products, new ideas - and the press and media remind us that there is always contention over methods, products and even plants. This collection, as well as acknowledging the passing of time in days, weeks, months and seasons, in some ways demonstrates that historically, time will show the truth of the old adage - the more things change, the more they remain the same.

Faith and Geoffrey Whiten
London

FOUR FUNDAMENTAL MAXIMS FOR MAKING A GARDEN

- Art must give place to Nature.

- Gardens should not be made dull and gloomy, by clouding them with thickets and too much cover.

- Gardens should not lay too open, so that it is needless to go into them to see them; you discover the whole at one view from the vestibule of the house without troubling yourself to walk in them.

- A Garden should always look bigger than it really is.

-Alexandre le Blond, *The Theory and Practice of Gardening*

NATURE IN GARDEN DESIGN

To build, to plant, whatever you intend,

To rear the column, or arch to bend,

To swell the terrace, or to sink the grot;

In all, let nature never be forgot.

But treat the goddess like a modest fair,

Nor over-dress, nor leave her wholly bare;

Let not each beauty ev'rywhere be spied,

Where half the skill is decently to hide.

-Alexander Pope

A GARDEN TAILORED TO ONE'S STATION IN LIFE

Although many men must be content with any plot of ground, of what form or quantity soever it be, more or less, for their garden, because a more large or convenient cannot be had to their habitation: Yet I persuade myself, that Gentlemen of the better sort and quality, will provide such a parcel of ground to be laid out for their Garden, and in such convenient manner, as may be fit and answerable to the degree they hold.

-Temple

To embellish the form of nature is an innocent amusement; and some praise must be allowed, by the most supercilious observer, to him who does best what such multitudes are contending to do well.

-Samuel Johnson

SOBERING INSTRUCTIONS ON THE IMPORTANCE OF A HEALTHY SITE FOR A HOUSE AND GARDEN

Too much caution cannot be exercised on this point. Data should be collected from the bills of mortality, by visits to the graveyards, by converse with the people, by observing the number and condition of the aged inhabitants, by the presence or absence of epidemic diseases, by the nature of the soil and subsoil, by the state of the crops, and by the physical stamina and moral condition of the inhabitants. No advantageous offer of a cheap plot of land; no contiguity to a town or railway; no desire even to be near your business, beyond what necessity requires, or to be near old friends; no theoretical fancies about the ameliorating influence upon climate of thorough drainage, or the effect of scientific cultivation, should induce anyone to build in an unhealthy locality.

-*The Beeton Book of Garden Management*

UNDERSTANDING JAPANESE GARDENS

In order to comprehend the beauty of a Japanese garden, it is necessary to understand - or at least to learn to understand - the beauty of stones. Not of stones quarried by the hand of man, but of stones shaped by nature only.

-Lafcadio Hearn

Anyone who with varying fortune is engaged in the creation of a garden may be likened to an explorer who embarks on a voyage through uncharted seas or unknown lands.

-A.N., *Gardeners Chronicle*, 1923

28

29

30

31

1

1685-Baptism of William Kent, landscape artist, at Bridlington, Yorkshire.

2

3

1923-Chamber of Horticulture Conference on methods of selling and distributing horticultural produce.

CHARLES LAMB TAKES UP GARDENING IN 1823

When you come Londonward, you will find me no longer in Covent Garden; I have a cottage in Colebrook Row, Islington... the New River (rather elderly by this time) runs (if a moderate walking pace can be termed) close to the foot of the house; and behind is a spacious garden with vines (I assure you); pears, strawberries, parsnips, leeks, carrots, cabbages... I am so taken up with pruning and gardening, quite a new sort of occupation to me. I have gathered my jargonels, but my winter pears are backward. The former were of exquisite raciness. I do now sit under my vine, and contemplate the growth of vegetable nature.

JOHNATHAN SWIFT ON GARDENERS

And he gave it for his opinion, that whoever could make two ears of corn or two blades of grass to grow upon a spot of ground where only one grew before, would deserve better of mankind, and do more essential service to his country than the whole race of politicians put together.

BACON ON THE VALUE AND PURE PLEASURE OF GARDENS

God Almighty first planted a garden. And indeed, it is the purest of human pleasures. It is the greatest refreshment to the spirits of man; without which, buildings and palaces are but gross handy-works; and a man shall ever see, that when ages grow to civility and elegance, men come to build stately than to garden finely; as if gardening were the greater perfection.

SNOW IN THE SUBURBS

Every branch big with it,
Bent every twig with it;
Every fork like a white web-foot;
Every street and pavement mute:

Some flakes have lost their way, and grope
    back upward, when
Meeting those meandering down they turn
    and descend again,
The palings are glued together like a wall,
And there is no waft of wind with the Fleecy
    fall.

A sparrow enters the tree,
Whereupon immediately
A snow-lump thrice his own slight size
Descends on him and showers his head and
    eyes,

And overturns him, And near inurns him,
And lights on a nether twig, when its brush
Starts off a volley of other lodging lumps
    with a rush.

The steps are a blanched slope,
Up which, with feeble hope,
A black cat comes, wide-eyed and thin;
    And we take him in.

-Thomas
Hardy

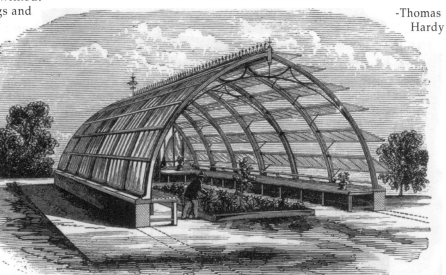

If you be not able, nor willing to hire a gardener, keep your profits to yourself, but then you must take all the pains.

-William Lawson, 1618

JANUARY

4

5

6

1975-Launch of Peter Seabrook's *"Dig This!"*, a weekly feature of BBC Television's Pebble Mill programme. This demonstrated how to have fresh, home-grown vegetables from a 10' x 12' plot every week of the year for less than £1.00 a year outlay on seeds and an hour a week's effort. It was hugely successful and led to both *"Dig This! Vegetable Guide"* and *"Peter Seabrook's Complete Vegetable Gardener Book"* which sold over a quarter of a million copies.

7

8

9

1729-Telfords of York supplied all the vegetable seeds for the season to Studley Royal Gardens, at a cost of £11. 8s. 2d.

10

LETTER FROM SIR JOSEPH BANKS TO A FELLOW NATURALIST, 15TH FEBRUARY 1794

My dear Sir George,

...Capt. Bligh succeeded in his Bread Fruit voyage beyond our most sanguine hopes. He brought near 1,000 Bread Fruit and other useful plants from the East to the West Indies and all the accounts I have since received prove them to be thriving in an extraordinary degree in their new climate.

...The nutmeg preserved in liquer which was forwarded to me in a bottle arrived in London Sept. 3rd. At that season of the year it is impossible to sow any seeds with hopes of success. We do not indeed venture after June as the dark and damp weather of winter is certain notwithstanding a sufficient heat is applied to destroy the cotyledones as soon as they rise from the earth. It is however safe in my possession unopened and will be sown with the utmost care and attention in March which is the earliest time we can venture to sow.

THE WARDIAN CASE

This small glass case in which plants can be grown indoors was the invention of Mr. B.N. Black, an eminent surgeon. It enabled plant collectors to send back home from their expeditions, plants and cuttings which would not otherwise have survived long sea voyages. The Wardian Case also became a fashionable accessory for the ornamental display of plants in Victorian sitting rooms.

Come into the garden, Maud,
For the blackbat, night, has flown,
Come into the garden, Maud,
I am here at the gate alone.
And the woodbine spices are wafted abroad,
And the musk of the roses blown.

-Tennyson

REGINALD FARRER ON SUCCESSFUL PLANT HUNTING...

Here, then, (in the Sino-Burmese Alps) in high happiness, I have been spending the summer, collecting flowers, and tending the local sick. Though this, indeed, is the last edge of nowhere, my own chief work has really lain almost over the edge... Up on the high passes overhead into China I have spent the chief of the summer in cloud that never lifted and rain that never ceased. It has been, indeed, a wonderful season.

...UNSUCCESSFUL PLANT HUNTING...

Very cold blew the wind along the topmost arete. And very cold was my mood, as I roamed its sharp dells of turf and examined its dorsal fins of rock, only to find nothing new whatever; far along I roamed, and up and down, and nowhere came on any better luck.

...AND THOSE WHO FAIL TO UNDERSTAND THE IMPORTANCE OF PLANT HUNTING EXPEDITIONS

The countless cross examinations I have undergone since my return at the hands of the more intelligent have left me with a conviction that people's prime interest in one's travel experiences lies in learning what one had to eat and drink.

11

12

1699-Appointment of James Sutherland as King's Botanist under a Warrant of William III. Sutherland was instrumental in creating the Royal Botanic Garden, Edinburgh.

13

14

15

1892-Great Sales of Imported Orchids held at Protheroe and Morris rooms in London. Orchids were extremely popular and sales were often held at prestigious auction houses.

16

17

SITUATIONS WANTED 1892

JOURNEYMAN in the Houses. Age 19. Edward Beckett, gardener to H.H. Gibbs MP, will be pleased to recommend a young man as above, who has lived under him the last five years. Strong, active and willing. W. Childs, The Garden, Aldenham House, Elstree.

HEAD GARDENERS: John Laing & Sons can at present recommend with every confidence several energetic and practical Men of tested ability and first-rate character. Ladies and Gentlemen in want of **GARDENERS** and **BAILIFFS** and **HEAD-GARDENERS** for first rate Establishments or Single-handed situations, can be suited and have full particulars by applying at Stanstead Park Nurseries, Forest Hill, London S.E.

TO GENTLEMEN etcetera. Young man wants a job on estate, as Carpenter etc. Used to Greenhouse building, repairing, glazing. A.F. 3 Bournemouth Terrace, Folkestone.

TO NURSERYMEN & FLORISTS - Advertiser seeks re-engagement as grower of soft-wooded stuff, Palms, Ferns etc. In or near London preferred. G. Baldwin, 2 Victoria Lane, Tottenham.

TO MARKET & FRUIT GROWERS. Manager - age 43, married; experienced in Grapes, Peaches, Tomatos, Cucumbers, Plants and Cut Bloom. Also outdoor fruit and vegetables. Excellent references. J.M. 1 Milligan Terrace, Leicester.

IMPROVER under a good gardener, bothy preferred. Age 19, five years experience. Good character. C. F. Bloomsbury Nursery, Timperley, Nr. Manchester.

Gardeners seem to be a class of men who are considered never to be so tired and run down that it is necessary to have a holiday.

-"An Old Stager", 1914

18

19

1970-The first *Gro-Bag* was launched by Fisons for the professional grower, and was followed by the launch of the consumer *Gro-Bag* in 1974.

20

21

22

1919-Death of George Bunyard V.M.H., a renowned fruit grower.

23

24

HOW TO DOUBLE DIG

This was previously called Bastard Trenching, but the term now generally accepted for it is Double Digging. To bring ground into good condition, it must be dug deeply and well in this manner:

Start by taking out a trench 2ft. wide, to the full depth of the good topsoil - usually the depth of the spade - across one end of the plot, and place this soil at the other end of the plot for filling the last trench. The loose soil or "crumbs" are then shovelled out and likewise carted to the other end.

When the "crumbs" have been removed from the first trench the subsoil should be broken up thoroughly to the full depth of the garden fork, at the same time mixing in any half-decayed vegetable refuse and manure available.

The next strip of similar width, 2ft., is then marked with the garden line (for convenience of measuring a 2ft. stick should be cut for each end), and the topsoil from this strip is then turned upside-down into the first trench, followed by the crumbs.

The subsoil is broken up and manured, and these operations repeated, trench by trench, until the whole plot has been dealt with and the last trench filled with the soil from the first.

-The Popular Encyclopaedia of Gardening, c. 1942

IN PRAISE OF DIRT AND DIGGING

The love of dirt is among the earliest of passions, as it is the latest. The love of digging in the ground (or of looking on while he pays another to dig) is as sure to come back to a man, as he is sure, at last, to go under the ground, and stay there. To own a bit of ground, to scratch it with a hoe, to plant seeds, and watch their renewal of life - this is the commonest delight of the race, the most satisfactory thing a man can do.

-Charles Dudley Warner, 1870

THE HORTICULTURAL APPLICATIONS OF MORTAR RUBBLE, 1946

When houses are demolished, the plaster and old mortar, made of lime and sand, are collected for use in the garden; this material is known as mortar rubble, old mortar or mortar waste. Mortar rubble is a mixture of sand and inactive chalk. On account of its non-caustic nature it is frequently used for potting composts; one part in four parts of loamy soil can be used in order to supply the compost with sand and carbonate of lime, thus keeping it porous.

Old mortar may be added freely to garden soils; it is most beneficial on heavy ground. It may be applied at any time of year, left on the surface, and dug in at leisure.

Among plants that like old mortar or mortar rubble are Carnation, Rose, Sweet Pea, Pea, Bean, many alpines, Cacti and succulents. It should be broken down finely for use in potting composts. If mortar rubble is left in the open it slowly disintegrates until it is sufficiently fine for general use.

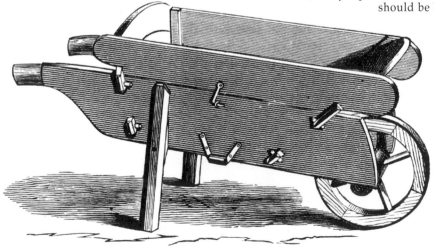

There is no ancient gentlemen but gardeners,
ditch-diggers and grave-makers
-Shakespeare

25

1993-Flower Show, R.H.S. Halls, Westminster, featuring Ornamental
Plant Competition and Botanical Paintings (two days).

26

27

28

29

1919-Royal Society of Arts lecture by the Controller of
Horticulture: "Food Production by Intensive Cultivation".

30

31

MAKE THE MOST OF YOUR GARDEN WITH BULLDOG TOOLS

The impressive Bulldog collection offers an unparalleled selection of quality hand tools for virtually every gardening task.

Bulldog acknowledges that just as every garden is different, so no two gardeners are the same. Therefore, the Bulldog horticultural portfolio offers five superb ranges of hand tools designed to meet the varying needs of the marketplace.

Designed with the discerning or professional gardener in mind the Bulldog Stainless range offers the ultimate in presentation and is an ideal gift for that special person. When used, the smooth surface discourages soil from clogging the tool heads, and after use can easily be cleaned.

Bulldog's firmly established Premier range is positioned as the ideal choice for the serious gardener and offers a combination of strength and durability. Its handcrafted products feature Bulldog's own unique formula of carbon manganese steel, with a hand-finished solid wood shaft and handle. Indeed, Bulldog offers a ten year guarantee on all Premier spades and forks.

Next there is the Bulldog Evergreen range.

The range is made up of 17 products which cover the majority of the needs of the gardener. Included in the range are spades and forks, both digging and ladies, lawn and garden rakes, dutch hoe, edging knife as well as border, lawn and hand shears, secateurs, loppers and weed forks and trowels.

A Bulldog spade is made in the Wigan factory

Look out also for the Country Manor range of tools combining good looks and value for money.

Finally, the Bulldog Popular range is manufactured with the price-conscious gardener in mind whilst still applying the same quality standards as the other ranges.

At Clarington Forge, Wigan, Bulldog Tools Ltd manufactures the finest range of high quality tools for the horticultural, agricultural and contractor markets. Established for over 200 years, the company has developed a unique combination of modern manufacturing methods and time-tested craftsmanship.

The high standard of finish and attention to detail is a reflection of the care taken with each tool through every stage of manufacture. Bulldog Tools manufacture to Quality Assurance Standard BS5750.

IF YOU THINK THERE'S NOTHING TO CHOOSE BETWEEN GARDEN TOOLS...

ONE garden tool may look very much like another,
but if you dig a little deeper you'll
unearth some very interesting facts about Bulldog tools.

UNIQUE CARBON MANGANESE STEEL

Bulldog tools, for example, are made from a unique steel
which Bulldog actually make themselves to ensure
lasting strength and resilience.

FINEST HARDWOOD HANDLE

Nothing less than the world's finest hardwood is good
enough for the shaft of a Bulldog tool,
making it a real pleasure to handle as you work.

THE BULLDOG SOCKET

The socket is potentially the weakest part of a spade or fork.
Some manufacturers ignore this fact and reduce the
length of the shaft hidden inside the socket to save cost.
Bulldog don't. Burying the shaft deeper and more securely
in the socket almost to the blade itself.

AN INVESTMENT IN QUALITY

The quality of Bulldog materials is matched only by the
meticulous standards of workmanship - standards
acknowledged and appreciated by professional and
discerning gardeners for over 200 years.

A BULLDOG RANGE THAT'S RIGHT FOR YOU

Bulldog offer four ranges; for discerning gardeners, there's
the strength of the Stainless range. Premier is perfect
for the serious gardener - while if you like to make gardening
a family affair, the Evergreen range is just right for you.
And for unbeatable value why not try the Popular range!
Available now from all good garden centres and
leading DIY retailers.

...IT'S TIME YOU DID SOME SPADE WORK

BULLDOG

Bulldog Tools Ltd., Clarington Forge,
Wigan WN1 3DD. Tel: 0942 44281

THE FINEST TOOLS ON EARTH

ALEXANDER POPE LISTS A CATALOGUE OF TOPIARY PLANTS BEING OFFERED BY LOCAL NURSERIES, HIS TONGUE FIRMLY IN HIS CHEEK

Adam and Eve in yew (Adam a little shattered by the fall of the tree of Knowledge in the great storm; Eve and the serpent very flourishing).

Noah's Ark in holly, the ribs a little damaged for want of water.

St. George in Box (His arm scarce long enough, but will be in a condition to stick the dragon by next April).

A green dragon of the same, with a tail of ground-ivy for the present. (NB - Those two are not to be sold separately). Edward the Black Prince in Cypress... A Queen Elizabeth in Phyllirea, a little inclining to the Green sickness, but full of growth... An old Maid of Honour in wormwood.

A topping Ben Johnson in Laurel.

Divers eminent modern poets in bays, somewhat blighted, to be disposed of a penny worth.

MR. CUTBUSH'S CUT BUSHES

In the Edwardian period, ornate garden ornament was very much in vogue - not least in the form of topiary. At the Royal International Horticultural Exhibition in 1912 individual items of topiary on show included clipped corkscrews, birds, dogs, sundials and gnomes, balls, columns and pyramids - even a complete picket style fence with a series of piers at regular intervals. The doyen of the art of topiary was acknowledged to be a Mr. Cutbush, thus prompting the fruits of his creativity to become known as *Mr. Cutbush's cut bushes*.

JOSEPH ADDISON RAILS AGAINST TOPIARY AND FORMALITY

Writers who have given us an account of China, tell us the inhabitants of that country laugh at the plantations of our Europeans, which are laid out by the rule and the line; because they say, anyone may place trees in equal rows and uniform figures. Our British gardeners... instead of humouring nature, love to deviate from it as much as possible. Our trees rise in cones, globes, and pyramids. We see the marks of the scissors upon every plant and bush. I do not know whether I am singular in my opinion, but for my part, I would rather look upon a tree in all its luxuriancy and diffusion of boughs and branches, than when it is cut and trimmed into a mathematical figure.

If I could put my woods in song
And tell what's there enjoyed,
All men would to my gardens throng,
And leave the cities void.

-R.W. Emerson, *My Garden*

FEBRUARY

1

1560-A Mr. Child started a seed shop in Pudding Lane in the City of London, near the site where the Great Fire started 100 years later. The Child's seed business survived for centuries and was eventually bought by Hurst's Seeds.

2

3

4

5

6

7

1991-Publication of the first edition of *BBC Gardeners' World Magazine*.

A RECIPE FOR THE PRESERVATION OF WOODEN PLANT LABELS

Thoroughly soak the pieces of wood in which they are made in a strong solution of sulphate of iron; then lay them, after they are dry, in lime water. This causes a formation of sulphate of lime (a very insoluble salt) in the wood, and the rapid destruction of the labels by the weather is thus prevented. Bast, mats, twine and other substances used in tying or covering up trees and plants, when treated in the same manner, are similarly preserved.

-The Beeton Book of
Garden Management

ON REMEMBERING PLANT NAMES

For those who have not got very good memories for the names of plants, I strongly recommend them, if they can draw, to make a little coloured sketch, however small, on the page of a gardening book next to the name of the plant. This will be found a great help to the memory; I began gardening so late in life that I had to get all the help I could.

-Mrs. C.W. Earle

RECOMMENDED MATERIALS FOR PLANT LABELS

- Lead
- Zinc
- Tin
- Deal
- Earthenware
- Horn
- Bone
- Ivory
- Leather

A range of zinc labels of various shapes could be procured from *Messrs. Deane and Co.* of King William Street, London Bridge. Temporary Labels were made from cardboard or coarse linen, with a brass eyelet hole through which string or raffia was passed for attachment to the plant. A label of more than usual strength and endurance was sold by *Messrs. Dennison and Co.* of Shoe Lane, Fleet Street.

ZINC GARDEN LABELS

At M is shown a border standard or rafter and wall pin in galvanized iron. It has a head like the handle of a fiddle-pattern spoon, and pierced with holes to allow of the attachment of a zinc label by means of wire. The following are the prices per 100 at which these articles are supplied:

A, 3s. 6d
B, 2s. 6d.
C, 2s. 6d.
D, 2s. 9d.
E, 1s. 9d.
F, 1s. 8d.
G, 1s. 8d
H, 1s. 2d.
K, 1s 9d.
L, 1s. 8d.

Yeat's Indelible Ink, an ink expressly prepared for writing on zinc labels, is supplied at 6d. per bottle.

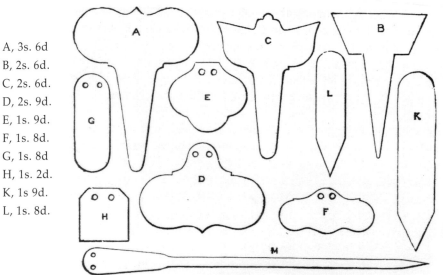

Don't rely too much on labels,
For too often they are fables.
                    -C.H. Spurgeon

FEBRUARY

8

1897-Mr. Roger Crompton purchased a nursery at Woodbridge, Suffolk, later to be known as Notcutts Nurseries and now run as part of a large and famous group of nurseries and garden centres by his grandson, Charles Notcutt.

9

10

1855-First winter meeting of the Horticultural Society at Regent Street, London.

11

12

13

14

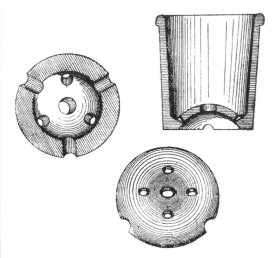

HOW TO MAKE A LOAM STACK

Turves should be cut in April and June when the grass is thick, and stacked with gaps between the sides and ends to allow aeration. As stacking proceeds, turves should be thoroughly wetted to ensure rapid rotting. Each 9 inch depth of turf alternates with a loose 2 inch layer of animal manure or half-composed straw. Suitable size of the stack is 6ft. high and 6-8 ft. wide. Cover the stack to keep off the rain. In about six months time the turves will be rotted and will have dried out ready for sterilization. The stack should be cut thinly by chopping down the stack from top to bottom with a spade, thus minimizing any variation in the quality of the turves and ensuring thorough mixing.

APPROXIMATE SIZES OF TRADITIONAL CLAY FLOWER POTS

Number to cast	Inside diameter at top (inches)	Outside Depth (inches)
72 (small)	$1^1/_2$	2
72 (medium)	2	3
72 (large)	$2^1/_2$	3
60 (small)	$2^3/_4$	$3^1/_4$
60 (medium)	3	$3^1/_2$
60 (large)	$3^1/_2$	4
54 (small)	4	$4^1/_4$
54 (large)	$4^1/_4$	$4^1/_2$
48 (small)	$4^3/_4$	$4^3/_4$
48	5	5
40	$5^1/_2$	$5^1/_2$
32	$6^1/_4$	$6^1/_4$
28	7	7
24	$7^1/_2$	$7^1/_2$
16	$8^1/_2$	$8^1/_2$
12	10	10
8	11	11
6	$12^1/_2$	$12^1/_2$
4	14	14
2	$15^1/_2$	$15^1/_2$
1	18	18

The 'number to cast' becomes the number by which that particular size of pot is identified e.g. 60s or 48s.

A BACKWARD SPRING

The trees are afraid to put forth buds.

And there is timidity in the grass;

The plots lie gray where gouged by spuds,

And whether next week will pass

Free of sly sour winds is the fret of each bush

Of barberry waiting to bloom.

Yet the snowdrop's face betrays no gloom,

And the primrose pants in its heedless push,

Though the myrtle asks if it's worth the fight

This year with frost and rime

To venture one more time

On delicate leaves and buttons of white

From the selfsame bough as last year's prime,

And never to ruminate on or remember

What happened to it in mid-December.

-Thomas Hardy

The love for plants in pots seems alive in all true gardeners.

-Viscountess Wolseley

FEBRUARY

15

16

17

18

19

1927-Frank Kingdom-Ward, plant explorer, published an account of his work with an Asian expedition in the Indo-Malayan jungle. Amongst the most interesting items seen were huge tree ferns.

20

21

Fair daffodils, we weep to see
You haste away so soon;
As yet the early-rising sun
Has not attain'd his moon,
　　Stay, stay,
Until the hasting day
　　Has run
But to the even-song;
And, having pray'd together, we
Will go with you along.

We have short time to stay, as you.

　　　　　　　　-Robert Herrick

THE MEANING OF A SNOWDROP

Legend has it that the snowdrop became the symbol for hope when Adam and Eve were expelled from the Garden of Eden. The snow was heavy, their journey was slow, and Eve was exhausted and despairing, believing that they were condemned to a future of hardship, without hope, and with endless winters. Suddenly an angel appeared and turned some flakes of snow into snowdrop flowers, proving that winter does end and eventually spring will arrive.

THE USES FOR VIOLETS

In medieval times, violet flowers were strewn on the floor of houses and on mattresses, and were used as a perfume to disguise the smell of unwashed bodies and clothes. Violets were also cooked with meat and game, eaten raw in salads and crystallized as sweets or cake decoration.

Queen Victoria always wore a posy of violets, and some 4,000 plants were grown under frames in the gardens at Windsor Castle to ensure a constant supply. In the 1850s, nearly one million bunches of sweet violets were sold in the streets of London each year.

　　　　　　　　-*The Lore of Flowers*,
　　　　　　　　　　Neil Ewart

Ran for sweethearts mad and died.
Love, in pity of their tears
And their loss in blooming years,
For their restless here-spent hours,
Gave them Heart's-ease turned to flowers.

　　　　　　　　-Robert Herrick

HOW THE PANSY GOT ITS NAME

The origin of the name Pansy is *pensée*, the French word for "thought". The flower is said to symbolise the thoughts of lovers, but also has sadder connections. Its old-fashioned name of *"Heart's Ease"* came from the tradition of planting the flower on the grave of a young girl who was said to have died of love.

METTAIS . SC

What's in a name? that which we call a rose
By any other name would smell as sweet.
-Shakespeare

FEBRUARY

22

23

1993-Flower Show at the R.H.S. Hall, Westminster, London. Features ornamental plant competition and botanical paintings.

24

25

1966-Levington compost was launched for both the professional grower and amateur gardener.

26

27

28

SUTTONS SEEDS

Suttons Seeds were founded in 1806 in Reading, Berkshire. Holders of the Royal Warrants for Her Majesty Queen Elizabeth and the Queen Mother, Suttons are now based in Torquay, Devon.

Suttons have an unrivalled reputation for quality and innovation, always providing the home gardener with an exciting range of flower and vegetable seed varieties. Suttons reputation for quality is due to the vigorous testing of all varieties, both in a laboratory and on extensive trial grounds in Ipplepen, Devon.

Each year Suttons introduce innovative new varieties and the very latest in new seed technology and 1993 is no exception. Suttons are introducing Supacoat Begonias, a real step forward for the home gardener. Natural Begonia seed is tiny and very difficult to handle. This new breakthrough not only increases the size of the seed, but also comes in a specially designed plastic phial which can be used as a seed sowing device simply by cutting the end of the tube. The varieties available are:- F1 Pin Up, F1 Non Stop, F1 Cocktail, F1 Devon Gems

Also new for 1993 are:-

GODETIA F1 SATIN MIXED

The world's first hybrid bedding godetia. It's early to flower and a dazzling range of colours will make a lovely display on the patio or in the bedding schemes.

SWEET PEA BOUQUET SERIES

There are four more exclusive new colours added to the range this year, Lavender, Navy Blue, Pink and Rose.

These multiflora types are ideal for garden decoration and as cut flowers. They have more flowers per stem than existing Spencer Sweet Peas.

CLARKIA BOTTAE PINK JOY

A lovely selection from an American Wild Flower which produces beautiful pink blooms on attractive foliage. A very easy-to-grow addition for your bedding schemes.

PANSY F1 IMPERIAL FROSTY ROSE

This is a stunning new introduction with a gorgeous face. It has been awarded the coveted Fleuroselect Gold Medal. It will make a perfect addition to any garden.

Some tasty new vegetable varieties to try are:-

LETTUCE TARGET

A new "Iceberg" Lettuce which produces solid hearts of crisp, tasty leaves. An exclusive for Suttons.

TOMATO F1 NIMBUS

A brand new variety which has been specially bred for its taste and high yield. It's ideal for growing organically and is resistant to Fusarium and Tomato Mosaic Virus.

CLIMBING FRENCH BEAN GOLDMARIE

An impressive new variety which produces delicious pale yellow flattened pods in profusion throughout the season.

MARROW F1 TIVOLI

Tivoli is an award winning variety which produces excellent cream skinned fruit. Use as Vegetable Spaghetti.

There are lots more new varieties for 1993, plus all of your favourites, too.

Supergrass !

Suttons have introduced a stunning new range of Lawn Seed

MIXTURES WITHOUT RYEGRASS

SUPREME
For a superb formal green lawn

GREENSHADOW
A fine grass mixture for areas of restricted sunlight

SUMMERDAY
For a low maintenance quality fine lawn

WEAR-REPAIR
A blend of quick growing seed for a fast repair

MIXTURES WITH RYEGRASS

SUMMERPLAY
A hard-wearing lawn for all the family

GREENGLADE
For shaded areas

EASYGREEN
For a tough evergreen lawn

WEAR-REPAIR
A blend of quick growing seed for a fast repair

INGREDIENTS OF JOHN INNES COMPOSTS

Seed Compost

		{Super 1ozs}	per bushel
	{2 loam}	{Chalk $^3/_4$oz}	
Parts by bulk	{1 peat} +	or	
	{1 sand}	{Super 2lbs}	per cubic yard
		{Chalk 1lb}	

Potting Composts

		{J.I. Base lb}	per bushel
	{7 loam}	{Chalk $^3/_4$oz}	
Parts by bulk	{3 peat} +	or	
	{2 sand}	{J.I. Base 5lbs}	per cubic yard
		{Chalk 1lb}	

Super = superphosphate of lime, 18% phosphoric acid

Chalk = ground chalk, ground limestone, limestone flour or whiting

Loam = sterilised loam

SEED TRAYS AND FLOWER POTS

A traditional nursery seed tray measures 14 x 8$^1/_2$ inches inside. Nine shallow trays of 2 inches, or six deep trays of 3 inches can be prepared from a bushel of soil.

The seed tray holds:

● 40 plants: 5 rows of 8 at 1$^3/_4$ x 1$^3/_4$ inches apart
● 54 plants: 6 rows of 9 at 1$^1/_2$ x 1$^1/_2$inches apart
● 60 plants: 6 rows of 10 at 1$^1/_2$ x 1$^1/_2$ inches apart

HARMONY AND ITS ROLE IN THE PROPAGATION OF TREES & SHRUBS

The fundamental principle governing success in the act of propagation is to utilise and not oppose the natural forces underlying plant growth. Once having determined the most effective method, whether it be natural or artificial, the whole operation must be conducted in a manner where the natural functions and processes of the subject are in complete harmony with the environment.

Among the various methods of propagation are:

● Open ground sowing
● Under-glass sowing
● Division
● Layering (general method)
● French-mound layering
● Cutting in open ground, coldframe, sun frame, bell-jars or under glass
● Eye cuttings
● Root cuttings
● Grafting
● Root grafting
● Budding

-From *Propagation of Trees, Shrubs & Conifers* by Wilfred G. Sheat, Horticulturist, Ministry of Transport, 1957

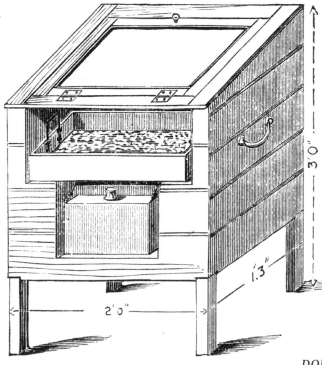

3' 0"

1.3"

2' 0"

DOBSON'S UNRIVALLED PROPAGATOR

Propagate, propagate, propagate.
                    -Rev. Charles Wolley Dod

1

1878-The Belgian government decreed a fixed course of training lessons for would-be professional gardeners, to include fruit-growing and market-gardening. The classes were held on Sundays to allow the maximum number of people to attend.

2

3

4

1960-Publication of the first edition of *Practical Gardening* magazine.

5

6

7

LINES WRITTEN IN EARLY SPRING

I heard a thousand blended notes,
While in a grove I sat reclined,
In that sweet mood when pleasant thoughts
Bring sad thoughts to the mind.

To her fair works did Nature link
The human soul that through me ran;
And much it grieved my heart to think
What man has made of man.

Through primrose tufts, in that green bower,
The periwinkle trailed its wreaths;
And 'tis my faith that every flower
Enjoys the air it breathes.

The birds around me hopped and played,
Their thoughts I cannot measure:-
But the least motion which they made
It seemed a thrill of pleasure.

The budding twigs spread out their fan,
To catch the breezy air;
And I must think, do all I can,
That there was pleasure there.

If this belief from heaven be sent,
If such be Nature's holy plan,
Have I not reason to lament
What man has made of man?

-William Wordsworth

Spring is come home with her world-wandering feet,
And all things are made young with young desires.
-Francis Thompson

8

9

10

11

12

13
1927-The United Horticultural Benefit and Provident Society advertised sickness and death insurance and saving schemes.

14
1993-Second day of the R.H.S. Orchid Show at the New Hall, Westminster, London.

What greater delight is there than to behold the earth apparelled with plants, as with a robe embroidered worke, set out with Orient pearls and garnished with great diversitie of rare and costly jewels?

-Gerard

THE PLEASURE OF FLOWERS

I always feel delighted when an object in nature brings up in one's mind an image of poetry that describes it from some favourite Author... The clown knows nothing of these pleasures... he knows they are flowers and just turns an eye on them and plods bye. Therefore as I said before to look on nature with a poetic eye magnifys the pleasure she herself being the very essence and soul of poetry.

-John Clare

ON THE DANGER OF TRANSPLANTING PAEONIES

The Paeony used to be called **"Aglaophotis"**, meaning brightly shining, in reference to dark seeds which were said to shine at night like a candle. Darker superstitions held that it was dangerous to pull up a paeony and anyone who touched a plant in an attempt to move it, would surely perish. It was therefore recommended that a string should be fastened to the plant at night and a hungry dog tied to the other end. The dog should be lured by the smell of roast meat set towards him and, in search of the food, would pull the Paeony up by the roots.

CUTHILL'S STRAWBERRIES:

The early Black prince 5s. per 100
The Late prince of Wales 7s. 6d.
per 100
They are sure and great bearers; they are best of all for preserving

A SELECTION OF MATERIALS FOR PROTECTING FRUIT AND BLOSSOM ON FRUIT TREES, AS RECOMMENDED IN 1890

Patent Cotton Net - made in pieces 50 yards long, and in three qualities.

Frigi Domo - made from prepared hair and wool. Lightweight, heat-saving and weatherproof.

Tiffany or Cotton Bunting - sold in a piece 40 yards long and also useful for greenhouse shading.

Scrim Canvas - especially "Willesden Rot-Proof Scrim" which was durable and water-repellent.

Old Bunting - made of wool used to make flags. Very narrow width.

Netting - available new or second-hand at 6d. per yard run.

THE SMALL CELANDINE

There is a flower, the lesser Celandine,

That shrinks, like many more, from cold and rain;

And, the first moment that the sun may shine,

Bright as the sun himself, 'tis out again!

When hailstones have been falling swarm on swarm,

Or blasts the green field and the trees distrest,

Oft have I seen it muffled up from harm,

In close self-shelter, like a Thing at rest.

-Wordsworth

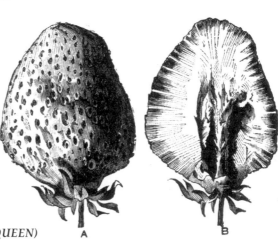

STRAWBERRY (BRITISH QUEEN)
A. Fruit B. Section.

A   B

MARCH

15

16

1993-Flower Show at the R.H.S. Halls, Westminster featuring Camellias, Rhododendrons and Daffodils.

17

18

19

1902-A Convention in Paris reached an international agreement for the protection of birds.

20

21

THE PRICE OF A PERFECT LAWN

A well-kept lawn adds immeasurably to the charm and beauty of a garden. It is attractive in itself, and affords the perfect setting for flowers, shrubs, ornamental plants and many garden features.

The perfect lawn cannot be made or maintained without some effort, however. Inattention as much as mismanagement can lead to deterioration. The lawn is ever open to weed invasion, and the perennial upkeep of an even, velvety sward of grasses calls for intelligent and regular care.

TASKS INVOLVED IN LAWN MANAGEMENT

- ✂ Mowing
- ✂ Edging
- ✂ Rolling
- ✂ Raking and Harrowing
- ✂ Switching
- ✂ Spiking and Forking
- ✂ Top-Dressing
- ✂ Fertilising
- ✂ Watering
- ✂ Earthworm Control
- ✂ Lawn Weed Control

COMMON LAWN TROUBLES

- ✂ Moss
- ✂ Fungal Disease
- ✂ Cortium Disease
- ✂ Fairy Rings
- ✂ Leatherjackets
- ✂ Ants

COMMON LAWN WEEDS

- ✂ Broadleaved Plantain
- ✂ Cat's-ear
- ✂ Creeping Buttercup
- ✂ Creeping Thistle
- ✂ Daisy
- ✂ Dandelion
- ✂ Dock
- ✂ Hawkbit
- ✂ Hawkweed
- ✂ Ribwort Plantain
- ✂ Shepherd's Purse

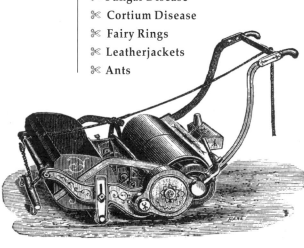

- The Popular Encyclopaedia of Gardening

Say, has some wet bird-haunted English lawn
Lent it the music of its trees at dawn?
                                    -Matthew Arnold

MARCH

22

1915-Launch of *Tomorite* tomato fertiliser, now a liquid but originally in solid form.

23

24

25

26

27

28

1919-War Horticultural Relief Fund Matineé, London Palladium.

VERSATILE LAWN CARE

Different types of gardeners treat their lawns in totally different ways. It all depends on the level of interest, the money in their pocket and the equipment they have available.

That is why ICI Garden Products make available many different forms of fertilizers and weedkillers.

USING A WATERING CAN

The favoured method for "pocket hand-kerchief" sized lawns is diluting products in a watering can. For quick, safe feeding add either Miracle-Gro Lawn Food crystals or ICI Lawncare Liquid Lawn Feed to the water, stir up and apply evenly. If broad-leaved weeds are a problem use Lawncare Liquid Weed & Feed instead for this will kill them off at the same time as greening the grass.

After application of a weedkiller, the watering can must be cleaned thoroughly.

USING A HOSE-END DILUTER

There are two automatic diluters to choose from. The 1 Litre size of Lawncare Liquid Feed comes complete with a hose end diluter for quick and easy treatment. For a versatile feeder which can later be used with Miracle-Gro Plant Food all round the garden then the Miracle-Gro Feeder is ideal. It automatically dissolves Miracle-Gro Lawn Food to feed the larger lawn in minutes.

BY HAND

For top quality grass and long-term feeding which lasts, then Lawncare Lawn Feed granules, available in cartons to treat 80 square yards is kinder to the environment.

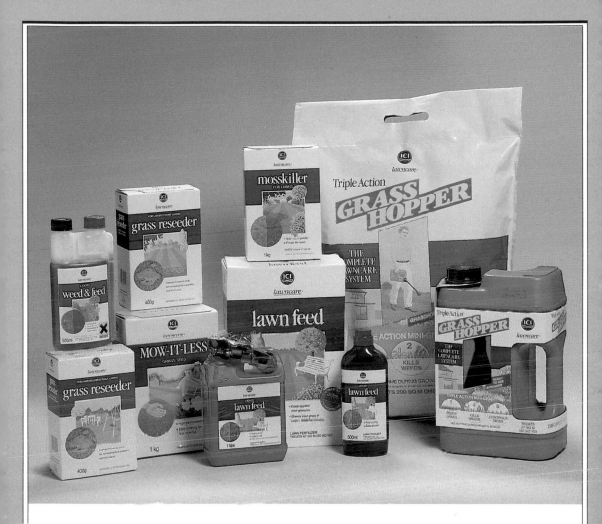

It contains a unique ingredient "Didin" which provides a phased release of nitrogen. The most popular selective lawn weedkiller is "Verdone" 2 and this can be diluted in water and applied through a watering can when the weeds are actively growing.

WITH A BUILT-IN SPREADER

For the all-in-one treatment of medium or larger lawns Tripe-Action "Grasshopper" offers a ready for use Spreader which makes lawn treatment as easy as walking. The granules feed the grass, get rid of lawn weeds and control moss all at the same time. There are refill boxes (80 sq. yards) and refill sacks (240 sq. yards) so that the largest lawn can be treated economically.

Garden Products

Fernhurst, Haslemere, Surrey GU27 3JE

Read the label before you buy: Use pesticides safely. Lawncare Liquid Weed & Feed contains dicamba, dichlorprop and MCPA. Triple-Action "Grasshopper" contains 2, 4-D, dicamba and ferrous sulphate. "Verdone" 2 contains mecoprop and 2, 4-D.

Products marked thus: "Grasshopper", are trade marks of Imperial Chemical Industries PLC. Miracle-Gro is a trade mark of Stern's Nurseries. Didin is a trade mark of SKW Trostberg AG.

Until 1830, lawns were generally cut either by men with scythes or grazed by sheep. But in that year, mechanisation came to grass cutting with the invention by Edward Beard Budding of a "machine for mowing lawns." Budding was an engineer in a textile factory and his patented design was first manufactured by a Mr. Ferrabee at Phoenix Works, Stroud in Gloucestershire. It was felt that the lawn mower offered to country gentlemen "amusing, healthy and useful exercise" - a theme that was taken up in 1841 by Mrs. Jane Loudon, who wrote in the *Ladies' Companion to the Flower Garden* that the lawn mower was now "particularly adapted for amateurs, affording an excellent exercise to the arms and every part of the body."

The earliest mowers had rotating blades, and on the lawns of large country houses they were drawn by horses. To avoid damage to the turf from the horses' hooves, they were fitted with specially designed leather boots. These were still in use in 1912, when Messrs H. Pattison & Co of Streatham advertised their "well known horse boots for use on lawns etc."

ROLLERS

Horses clad in boots were also used to draw lawn rollers, although these have a much longer history than the mower. As early as 1259, the newly-laid turf at the Palace of Westminster was rolled with a marble roller and in the seventeenth and eighteenth centuries, rollers were still generally made from stone, shaped into cylindrical form.

THE DEVELOPMENT OF THE LAWN MOWER

As might be expected, the ease and convenience offered by the lawn mower caused it to be embraced by professional and amateur gardeners with great enthusiasm. By 1890, so many different types and models were available that the *Beeton Book of Garden Management* noted: "Mowing machines are as numerous as sewing machines, and where there are so many that are good, it is difficult, if not impossible, to assign the palm of excellence to any particular machine."

Among those on the market were:

The "Archimedean" American Lawn Mower (light, simple, not likely to get out of order, works well on slopes).

The "New Automaton" Lawn Mower (awarded a Silver Medal at the Inventions Exhibition of 1855 - graceful design, produces a velvety surface).

The "Easy" Lawn Mower (large sizes can be worked with facility on account of its lightness. Supplied by all ironmongers or Messrs Selig, Sonnenthal, Queen Victoria St., London EC).

The Patented "Excelsior" Lawn Mower (an American machine made at Newburgh, New York. Suited for large lawns and tennis courts on account of closeness, evenness and rapidity).

I hold that nothing unsightly should be seen in the garden.

-Gertrude Jekyll

MARCH/APRIL

29

30

31

1

1730-One of the earliest newspaper adverts for a nurseryman appeared in the *York Courant*, where Samuel Smith advertised his auriculas, anemones, ranunculus and tulips.

2

3

4

The Royal Horticultural Society was founded in 1804. Among its founding members were John Wedgwood, who preferred gardens to the family pottery. William Forsyth, gardener to King George III and Sir Joseph Banks, the eminent plant hunter and scientist. Banks wrote: "I know of no trade that conceals so many branches of knowledge as that of a gardener, and few subjects where the public will be more benefited by the disclosures which such a society will occasion."

many new introductions brought to Britain by plant hunters from China, India, South America and the West Indies. Six years later a Horticultural Fete was held there, with refreshments in marquees, displays of plants and accompaniment of a military band. This developed into four flower shows at Chiswick each year - all of which were hugely popular and successful. Then twenty acres of land at Kensington were developed as a venue for exhibitions and a show garden, but in 1888 new arrangements had to be made.

EXHIBITION EXTRAORDINARY in the HORTICULTURAL ROOM.

The first exhibit shown to a Society meeting was not a flower, but a potato which would keep well through the winter. At the Anniversary Dinner each year, gardeners vied to display the biggest and best selection of fruits grown under glass - especially pineapples. By 1858, awards to plants were introduced, as guidance to gardeners considering the worth of new introductions.

HORTICULTURAL FETES
In 1821 the garden at Chiswick House was developed by the Society as a show-piece and training centre, and a place to grow the

SHOWS AT TEMPLE GARDENS
Plans were made for an outdoor show to be held under canvas at the Embankment Gardens of the Inner Temple, close to Charing Cross. *The Gardener's Chronicle* reported: "On entering the long tent with its fine display of herbaceous plants and 'market stuff' the visitor could scarcely refrain from an exclamation of delight and surprise." The show became an annual event, but the noise of the band and the smell of refreshments and general disruption made for strained relations with the Templars and so the idea for a completely new exhibition at Chelsea was originated.

If you would be happy all your life, plant a garden.

-Chinese proverb

APRIL

5

6

7

8

1993-First day of the International Spring Gardening Fair, a new event to be held at Wembley, London.

9

10

11

1993-Easter Sunday. Traditionally one of the busiest days of the gardening year.

THE HANGING GARDENS OF BABYLON

HOW THE HA-HA GOT ITS NAME

At present we frequently make thorough-views called *Ha Ha*, which are openings in the walls, without grills to the very level of the walks, with a large and deep ditch at the foot of them, lined on both sides to sustain the earth, and prevent the animals getting over, which surprises the eye upon coming near it, and makes one cry *Ha! Ha!* from whence it takes its name.

-The Theory and Practice of Gardening, 1709

REGINALD FARRER ON THE FRAUDULENCE OF THE WILD GARDEN

The ordinary wild garden is the very worst and most extravagant of frauds, requiring a supervision no less incessant or close than any parterre or border... I hate the sight of respectable elderly persons doddering whole days through the "wild garden" and picking up a weed an hour, so that ultimately the whole place has an air of spick and spanness.

A GARDEN THAT CAUSES AMUSEMENT

I am one, you must know, who am looked upon as a humourist in gardening. I have several acres about my house, which I call my garden, and which a skilful gardener would not know what to call.

-Addison

HAMPTON COURT PALACE GARDEN

Labour employed in 1530:

Five labourers (men) paid fourpence per day

Fifteen weeders (women) paid threepence per day

Tools purchased in 1553: (from the Accounts)

Item, for three iron rakes serving for the King's new garden at 6d. the piece, 18d.

Item, for a hatchet serving for the said garden, 6d.

Item, for three new knives to shred the quicksets in the new garden at 3d., the piece, 9d.

Item, for six pieces of round line to measure and set forth the new garden, 12d.

Item, for two cutting hooks, 2s.

Item, for two cutting knives, 4d.

Item, for two rakes, 16d.

Item, for two chisels, 6d.

Item, for a grafting saw, 4d.

A garden is such an individual affair - it should show so distinctly the idiosyncrasy of its owner.
                                    -Reginald Blomfield

12

1993-Last day of the International Spring Gardening Fair.

13

14

1864-Marriage of Theresa Villiers to Charles Earle. As Mrs. C.W. Earle, she took up gardening in middle age and wrote the hugely successful *Pot-Pourri from a Surrey Garden* and other books.

15

16

1879 and 1913-Two Presidents of the Royal Horticultural Society - father and son - were born. Lord Henry Aberconway and Lord Charles Aberconway both fulfilled this role for over twenty years. Their garden at Bodnant is one Britain's most celebrated, particularly for its Rhododendrons.

17

18

When you are tired of herbaceous plants, let the jobbing gardener keep the border tidy, and you will soon be rid of the obnoxious lilies, phloxes, ranunculuses, anemones, hollyhocks, paeonies and pansies, without the painful labour of pulling them up and burning them.

-Shirley Hibberd

HERBACEOUS PLANTS IN MINIATURE

Advice from Jason Hill: "Those who have only the smallest area that can be called a garden, or even no garden at all, need not be quite helpless in their envy of the sumptuous full-dress herbaceous border, for there is a good handful of jewel-bright little herbaceous plants which can be composed into a picture in a tiny bed, a stone sink, egg-crock or a stout packing-case gaily painted."

A PRACTICAL APPROACH TO THE FLOWER BORDER FROM H.E. BATES

I am not a purist where borders are concerned. My sole purpose is to achieve the longest possible display of colour - virtually for nearly half the year - with the minimum of labour. My border therefore must be totally uncluttered by subjects which, however beautiful, have short lives... I call a plant excellent when it has the following virtues; that of being able to stand on its own legs without stakes, of producing flowers of great beauty for weeks on end and of showing incontestable grace of form.

GERTRUDE JEKYLL'S PRACTICAL ADVICE ON HERBACEOUS BORDERS

A good hardy flower border cannot be made all at once. Many of the most indispensable perennials take two, three or even more years to come to their strength and beauty. The best way is to plant the border by a definite plan, allowing due space for the development of each plant. Then, for the first year or two, a greater number of half-hardy annuals and biennials than will eventually be needed should be used to fill the spaces that have not yet been taken up by the permanent plants.

On first going into a garden one knows by instinct, as a hound scents the fox, if it is going to be interesting or not.

-Mrs. C.W. Earle

19

20

1993-Flower Show at R.H.S. Halls, Westminster featuring Daffodils and Tulips.

21

1637-Collapse of the tulip market in Holland, putting an end to the tulip-mania that had gripped the country for some three years, with bulbs being sold at hugely inflated prices.

22

1993-Harrogate Spring Show, Valley Gardens, Harrogate, Yorkshire (three days).

23

24

1993-14th World Orchid Conference and Show, Glasgow (until May 2nd).

25

SHIRLEY HIBBERD ON THE DESIGN OF THE PARTERRE

Geometric gardens may be designed on paper by selecting some part of the pattern of a carpet or wallpaper, or by placing a few bits of coloured paper in the kaleidoscope, and then copying the scheme so produced. Numbers of designs have been obtained in that way, and about one in a hundred have actually turned out worthy; the rest were not worth the paper they were drawn on.

...AND ON CIRCULAR BEDS

The common repetition, on the margins of lawns in private gardens, of circular beds containing standard roses, surrounded by geraniums, verbenas, and other such stuff, is ineffective and puerile.

FOUR ESSENTIALS

In every Garden Four Things are necessary to be provided for, Flowers, Fruit, Shade and Water, and whoever lays out a Garden without all these, must not pretend it in any perfection. It ought to lie to the best parts of the House, or to those of the Master's commonest Use, so as to be but like one of the Rooms out of which you step into another.

-Sir William Temple

WILLIAM GILPIN'S ADVICE ON THE ARRANGEMENT OF FLOWER BEDS

In what may be termed a free disposition of flower-beds, the first care should be to avoid the spottiness which must result from putting a bed wherever room can be found for it.

CREATIVE FENCING IDEAS

Those persons who have travelled in Holland and Belgium have no doubt noticed the neat manner in which small enclosures of land are separated from each other by their thrifty and industrious owners. The hedges are trained along stakes and rods placed for the purpose, and to these the plants of which they are composed are tied with pieces of osier. In this way every slender branch is laid in, and as they are made to cross each other frequently, a regular network is formed. These hedges, when in leaf, are very close and tight, they take up very little room, and form scarcely any harbour for small birds. Many of our ornamental plants might be thus trained to form hedges - the Cydonia Japonica, for instance, which is close, quick-growing, and bears a most beautiful flower. This plant is as hardy as any native British plant, and very easily propagated.

-A Victorian Writer

HUMPHREY REPTON ON THE UNDESIRABILITY OF WIDE, EMPTY PLACES

A large extent of ground without moving objects, however neatly kept, is but a melancholy scene. If solitude delight, we seek it rather in the covert of a wood, or the sequestered alcove of a flower-garden, than in the open lawn of an extensive pleasure-ground. I have therefore frequently been the means of restoring acres of useless garden to the deer or sheep, to which they more properly belong.

A parterre demands talent, and that is not always available.
    -Shirley Hibberd

26

1914-It was announced that, at a sale of books at Sotheby's, the following had been disposed of: First edition of *Gerard's Herbal*, 1597 for £3. 5s.0d.; 1656 edition of *Parkinson's Paradisi in Solo, Paradisus Terrestris* for £6. 0s. 0d.

27

28

29

30

1

1958-Notcutts opened its first garden centre at Woodbridge, one of the earliest garden centres to commence in Britain. Other pioneers included Russells, Wyevale and Christchurch.

2

1884-The first edition of *Amateur Gardening* magazine was published, promising to be "generally useful".

Are you one of the 15 million households in the United Kingdom which owns a hosepipe, but finds the handling and storage of it awkward and unsightly?

New from Hozelock, the gardener's most popular supplier of gardening watering products - the space-saving Wall Mounted Hose Reel. This unique product is new for 1993 and is available with or without hose at all good garden centres and DIY stores.

The Wall Mounted reel is a complete hose management system designed to make using a hose as effortless as possible. The water flows through the hose inside the reel, saving work and keeping your home and garden tidy.

Use the hose of your choice, up to a maximum of 50 metres long. Hozelock supply a wide range of hoses, hose connectors and accessories to create a practical system for using the hose for a variety of household needs. The Hozelock "quick-connect" system allows you to connect and disconnect water guns, sprayers and sprinklers to your hose with a click!

The secret of the new hose reel is the Hose Guide which allows the hose to unwind in any direction - just thread the hose through and use as much as you need in any part of the garden. The reel can be mounted in a convenient place to be used both for watering the garden and washing the car or caravan.

When you are finished with the hose, the precision engineered central bearing guarantees smooth and easy rewinding - there's even a place to store your hose ends on the reel.

At the end of the season the reel lifts off a specially designed bracket for storage as necessary. Hozelock recommend that the flow-thru design products such as the Wall Mounted Hose reel are stored away from frost.

Made in Britain

Hozelock Ltd., Haddenham, Aylesbury, Buckinghamshire HP17 8JD

NEW FOR 1993

THE WALL MOUNTED HOSE REEL

HOZELOCK

A COTTAGE FLOWER GARDEN

Nearer the house was a portion given up entirely to flowers, not growing in beds or borders, but crammed together in an irregular square, where they bloomed in half-wild profusion. There were rose bushes there and lavender and rosemary and a bush apple-tree which bore the little red and yellow streaked apples in later summer, and Michaelmas daisies and red-hot pokers and old-fashioned pompom dahlias in autumn and peonies and pinks already budding.

An old man in the village came one day a week to till the vegetable garden, but the flower garden was no one's special business... the flowers grew just as they would in crowded masses, perfect in their imperfection.

-Flora Thompson

REGINALD BLOMFIELD'S selection of flowers to contrast with the horrors of a nursery gardener's catalogue:

❀ Gillyflowers (pinks)
❀ Columbines
❀ Sweet Williams
❀ Sweet Johns
❀ Hollyhocks
❀ Marigolds
❀ Ladies' Slipper
❀ London Pride
❀ Bergamot
❀ Love-in-a-Mist
❀ Bachelor's Buttons

THE ENGLISH COTTAGE GARDEN

English cottage gardens are never bare and seldom ugly. Those who look at sea or sky or wood see beauty that no art can show; but among the things made by man nothing is prettier than an English cottage garden, and they often teach lessons that 'great' gardeners should learn, and are pretty from snowdrop time till the Fuchsia bushes bloom nearly into winter. We do not see the same thing in other lands...

-William Robinson

1 *Caryophyllus maximus rubro varius.* The great old Carnation or gray Hulo. 2 *Caryophyllus maior rubro & albo varius.* The white Carnation. 3 *Caryophyllus albo rubens.* The Camberfine or the Pookeflower. 4 *Caryophyllus Caryo foliatus.* The faire made of Kent. 5 *Caryophyllus Sabaudicus aureus.* The bluſh Sauadge. 6 *Caryophyllus X erampelinus.* The Greenfine Carnation. 7 *Caryophyllus diſtus Grimes.* The Grimſto or Prince. 8 *Caryophyllus albus maior.* The great white Gilloflower. 9 *Elegans Herina Bradſbury.* Maſter Bradilus wee dainty Lady.

A SELECTION OF PINKS

48

I always thought a kitchen garden a more pleasant sight than the finest orangery, or artificial greenhouse.

-Joseph Addison

3

4

5

6

7

1892-International Horticultural Exhibition, Earls Court.
1993-Malvern Spring Gardening Show (three days).

8

9

1826-Joseph Paxton started work for the Duke of Devonshire at Chatsworth, where he built the famous Great Conservatory.

BEFORE SUBMERSIBLE PUMPS

John B. Papworth describes how to make a fountain in about 1825: "To execute a simple form of fountain it is necessary to be in possession of a body of water at a sufficient height to produce the jet, and it must be something higher than the altitude proposed, because of the resistance the jet meets with, and amongst others, from the pressure of the air, and in striking against its descending waters: the aperture at which the water escapes must be proportioned to the height of the reservoir, and to the diameter of the conducting pipes."

SOME SUGGESTIONS FOR INTERESTING FOUNTAINS

I. The Ball raised by a Spout of Water

II. The Water representing a double Glass, the one over the other.

III. A Dragon or such like, casting Water out of its mouth, as it runs round on the Spindle.

IV. A Crown casting Water out of several Pipes as it runs round.

V. A Statue of a Woman, that at the turning of a private Cock, shall cast Water out of her Nipples in to the Spectators Faces.

VI. The Royal Oak with Leaves, Acorns and Crowns dropping, and several small spouts round the top.

-J.W. Gent, *Systema Horticultura*

INSTRUCTIONS FOR MAKING A FISH POND

You shall dig your Pond not above eight foot deepe, and so as it may carry not above six foot of water. You shall pave all the bottome, and backes of the Pond, with large sods of Flotgrasse, which naturally growes under the water, for it is a great feeder of Fish: and you shall lay them very close together, and pinne them downe fast with small stakes and windings. You shall upon one side of the Pond, in the bottome, stake fast divers battens of Faggots of brushwood wherein your fish shall cast their spawne, for that will defend it from destruction; and at another end you shall lay sods upon sods, with grasse sides together, in the bottome of the Pond, for that will nourish and breed Eales; and if you sticke sharp stakes slant-wise by everies side of the Pond, that will keepe thieves from robbing them.

-Gervase Markham, Cheap and Good Husbandry, 1614

THE DUBIOUS TASTE OF FOUNTAINS IN SMALL GARDENS

The great objection to fountains as garden decorations is to be found in the fact that they cannot always be in operation, and that they must be set in action like a musical box... in small gardens the introduction of a fountain savours somewhat of pretension. A tank or basin for the display of water lilies and aquatic plants is a different thing altogether, but it should be kept scrupulously clean, and constructed without the dumb-waiter-like centre piece, surmounted by the inevitable figure of a boy holding an erect squirt, which is seldom brought into requisition.

-The Beeton Book of Garden Management

Few architectural embellishments have so interesting an effect as fountains.

-John B. Papworth

10

11

12

13

1913-The Ministry of Agriculture announced a scheme to convert town refuse to fertiliser.

14

15

16

1914-Announcement of the completion of a new public garden at Kensal Town, donated by Mr. Horniman.

THE ROYAL INTERNATIONAL HORTICULTURAL EXHIBITION, 1912

This - the immediate forerunner to the Chelsea Flower Show - was held in the grounds of the Royal Hospital as a one-off, spectacular opportunity to display the best of British and international horticulture. Features of the show included:

☙ A vast marquee of nearly four acres and sundry small pavilions - all supplied by Piggot Bros.

☙ Plumbing, surface drains and electric lighting to serve almost the whole area, with water-carts in case of dry weather.

☙ Post office, telephones, St. John Ambulance Post, refreshment facilities including a first-class luncheon marquee with full waiter service.

☙ Visit by a large Royal party including King George, Queen Mary and their Royal Highnesses the Archduke and Archduchess Franz Ferdinand of Austria.

☙ A specially heated marquee devoted to orchids, where on the opening day gentlemen were required to wear tails rather than the customary morning dress, in recognition of the orchid as the aristocrat of plants.

☙ Exhibits of flowers, fruit and vegetables of every description.

☙ Exhibits of garden sundries, greenhouses, greenhouse boilers and ventilating gear.

☙ Full-scale gardens, especially rock gardens ranging from the expert and ambitious to the crude and simple.

☙ Displays of garden ornaments, especially in the fashionable Oriental style. Liberty's of Regent Street showed old bronze lanterns, Japanese arches, gate posts, storks and bamboo gates and bungalows - all romantically illuminated by quaint Oriental lanterns suspended from the roof of the stand.

The Exhibition was a great success and donated a large profit to charities. The scene was set for a new venue at Chelsea for the Royal Horticultural Society's show each May.

17

1855-Founding of the Society for the Improvement of Horticulture in the colony of New South Wales.

18

19

20

21

22

1914-Lightning destroyed an Atlas Cedar in Kew Gardens.

23

They think a murderer's heart would taint
Each simple seed they sow.
It is not true! God's kindly earth
Is kindlier than men know,
And the red rose would but blow more red,
The white rose whiter blow.

But neither milk-white rose nor red
May bloom in prison-air;
The shard, the pebble, and the flint,
Are what they give us there:
For flowers have been known to heal
A common man's despair.

So never will wine-red rose or white,
Petal by petal, fall
On that stretch of mud and sand that lies
By the hideous prison-wall,
To tell the men who tramp the yard
That God's son died for all.

            -Oscar Wilde, from *The Ballad
of Reading Gaol*

WEATHERS

I

This is the weather the cuckoo likes,
    And so do I;
When showers betumble the chestnut spikes,
    And nestlings fly:
And the little brown nightingale bills his best,
And they sit outside at "The Travellers' Rest",
And maids come forth sprig-muslin drest,
And citizens dream of the south and west,
    And so do I.

II

This the weather the shepherd shuns,
    And so do I;
When beeches drip in browns and duns,
    And thresh, and ply;
And hill-hid tides throb, throe on throe,
And meadow rivulets overflow,
And drops on gate-bars hang in a row,
And rooks in families homeward go,
    And so do I.
           -Thomas Hardy

A FIRM ADMONITION FOR LOVERS OF FLOWERS

Flowers through their beauty, variety of colour, and exquisite form, do bring to a liberal and gentlemanly mind, the remembrance of honesty, comeliness, and all kinds of virtues: for it would be an unseemly and filthy thing (as a certain wise man sayeth) for him that doth look upon and handle fair and beautiful things, to have his mind not fair, but filthy and deformed.

        -From *Gerard's Herbal*

Flowers seem intended for the solace of ordinary humanity.

-Ruskin

24

1912-The Royal International Horticultural Exhibition was held at Chelsea. It was one of the most important horticultural events this century and was accompanied by a whole series of international conferences.

25

1993-Chelsea Flower Show, Royal Hospital, Chelsea (25th & 26th, R.H.S. members only; 27th & 28th public entry).

26

27

28

29

30

The Wonderful and Magical World of Water Gardening

There is probably no aspect of Gardening that offers greater scope for enterprise, imagination and enjoyment than a water garden. Trident have a team of experts and pioneers in the field which makes them the most experienced in the market place.

A FASCINATING FOCAL POINT

Water gardens introduce a fascinating focal point. An active pool reflects the sunlight and creates feelings of relaxation and pleasure. Fish swim lazily beneath the surface in varied colours, sizes and shapes. Lillies as colourful as nature's best decorate the borders. Marginal plants flourish in and besides the water's edge. A dancing fountain or cascading waterfall lends life and sound. When night falls lighting provides a magical transformation of the wonderful world of water gardening. Thus Trident Water Garden Products brochure is the key to the bright world of water gardening.

A WORK OF ART

Now it is easy to install a pond or stream and thereby broaden the garden's horizons immeasurably. Indeed, you do not even need a garden at all. Your water garden can be on a terrace, patio, balcony, in fact anywhere where you've got a few spare square feet. Your water garden is destined to be a work of art, fashioned by you and nature in collaboration to bring life, movement, reflections and colour by day and night

through the year. A water garden can take many forms. It can be sunken or raised. It can be a rigid pool in Glass fibre and HDP (High Density Polyethylene). Alternatively it can be made by use of a flexible liner. These liners are available in many thicknesses, sizes and materials and provide many years of trouble free pleasure and service. No size is too small or too large. The only limitation is your imagination.

BRINGING YOUR CALL TO LIFE

When the structural work is completed the pleasant task of bringing your pool to life begins. This is done by installing a pump either submersible or surface mounted. A pump will operate a fountain, waterfall or filter, or a combination of any of these. Trident have a full range of submersible and surface mounted pumps to suit any installation.

THE FINAL SPARKLE OF INSPIRATION

The final sparkle of inspiration comes in the form of water gardening ornaments. An astonishing range is available in various shapes, sizes and colours guaranteed to glitter in the sunlight. They are available from concrete to marble, resembling humans, animals or creatures of mythology. Once again reflecting on the Wonderful and Magical World of Water Gardening.

You love the Roses - so do I. I wish
The sky would rain down Roses, as they rain
From off the shaken bush. Why will it not?
Then all the valley would be pink and white
And soft to tread on. They would fall as light
As feathers, smelling sweet; and it would be
Like sleeping and yet waking, all at once!

-George Eliot

HARRY WHEATCROFT

Harry Wheatcroft started growing roses in 1919, and became known variously as **"Mr. Rose"**, **"The King of Roses"** and **"The Prince of Rose Growers"**. His nursery, run with his brother, Alfred, represented the French grower, Meilland and introduced to Britain *Peace*, *Tzigane*, *Queen Elizabeth*, *Super Star* and *Fragrant Cloud* and many others. With his large moustache and flamboyant style, he was once declared "Best Dressed Man of the Year", but when he launched a brilliant orange rose called *Harry Wheatcroft* in 1972, the RHS Journal noted: "We were in fact undecided whether Mr. Harry Wheatcroft has raised a rose to suit his style in sartorial accessories or whether he had dressed for the occasion to match the rose."

NATIONAL ROSE SOCIETY RULES FOR JUDGING ROSES, 1878:-

POINTS:

Where points are necessary they shall be allotted as follows:

1. Three points shall be given for the best bloom; two for mediums; one for those not so good, but not enough to cast out; and an extra point for a very superior bloom.

2. One point shall be taken off the box for every case of decided badness.

3. Teas and Noisettes shall have no special favour shown to them as such.

DEFINITIONS:

1. A Bloom or Truss shall be taken to mean a Rose, with or without buds and foliage, as cut from the tree.

2. A good Rose must have form, size, brightness, substance, foliage, and be at the time of judging in the most perfect phase of its possible beauty.

3. A bad Rose - All blooms and trusses shall be considered bad that have faulty shape, confused centre, or faded colour; and which are either undersized, or over-sized to the extent of coarseness; or of over-blooming.

4. Form shall imply petals abundant, and of good substance, regularly and gracefully disposed within a circular symmetrical outline.

5. Brightness shall include freshness of colour, brilliancy and purity.

Roses are red, violets are blue;
But they don't get around like the dandelions do.
-Slim Acres

MAY/JUNE

31

1

2

3

1618-John Tradescant, famous plantsman and importer of exotic plants, set sail for Russia with Sir. Dudley Digges, an ambassador for James I. Tradescant observed many plants including Ribes, Roses, Hellbores, Herbs and Strawberries.

4

5

1952-Mr. Harold Hillier took up residence in Jermyns House, Ampfield, Hampshire, the garden of which was to become the Hillier Arboretum.

6

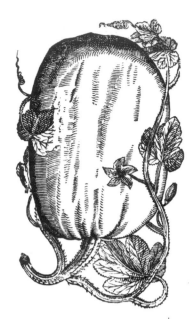

POMPIONS FROM GERARD'S HERBAL

VICTORIAN COTTAGE LIFE:
Gardens & Allotments, Flowers & Vegetables

On light evenings, after their tea-supper, the men worked for an hour or two in their gardens or on the allotments. They were first class gardeners and it was their pride to have the earliest and best of the different kinds of vegetables. They were helped in this by good soil and plenty of manure from their pigsties; but good tilling also played its part. They considered keeping the soil constantly stirred about the roots of growing things the secret of success and used the Dutch hoe a good deal for this purpose. The process was called "tickling". They grudged no effort and never seemed to tire. Often, on moonlight nights in spring, the solitary fork of some one who had not been able to tear himself away would be heard and the scent of his twitch fire smoke would float at the windows. It was pleasant, too, in summer twilight, perhaps in hot weather when water was scarce, to hear the swish of water on parched earth in a garden - water which has been fetched from the brook a quarter of a mile distant. "It's no good stintin' the 'land'", they would say. "If you wants anything out you've got to put summat in, if 'tis only elbow grease." The allotment plots were divided into two, and one half planted with potatoes and the other half with wheat or barley. The garden was reserved for green vegetables, currant and gooseberry bushes, and a few old-fashioned flowers. The women never worked in the vegetable gardens or on the allotments, even when they had their children off hand and had plenty of spare time, for there was a strict division of labour and that was 'men's work'. Victorian ideas, too, had penetrated to some extent, and any work outside the home was considered unwomanly. But even that code permitted a woman to cultivate a flower garden, and most of the house had at least a narrow border beside the pathway. As no money could be spared for seeds or plants, they had to depend upon roots and cuttings given by their neighbours, and there was little variety; but they grew all the sweet old-fashioned cottage garden flowers, pinks and sweet williams and love-in-a-mist, wallflowers and forget-me-nots in spring and hollyhocks and Michaelmas daisies in autumn.

As well as their flower garden, the women cultivated a herb corner, stocked with thyme and parsley and sage for cooking, rosemary to flavour the home-made lard, lavender to scent the best clothes, and peppermint, pennyroyal, horehound, camomile, tansy, balm and rue for physic. They made a good deal of camomile tea, which they drank freely to ward off colds, to soothe the nerves, and as a general tonic.

-Flora Thompson, *Lark Rise*

If I have pleasure in a flower-garden, I have in a kitchen-garden too.

-William Hazlitt

7

8

9

10

1848-Mr. Fortune leaves Chelsea Botanic Gardens to go to China to procure tea plants for the East India Company.

11

12

13

MOTTOS TO BE FOUND ON SUNDIALS

Time was made for slaves, men say;
Yet free men ask the time of day

Believe me mortals when I say
The past is what we make today

Let others tell of storms and showers
I'll only count the sunny hours

A clock the time may wrongly tell;
I, never, if the sun shine well

A moment - mark how small a space
The dial shows upon the face;
Yet waste but one - and you will see
Of how great moment it may be

Horum sole negante nego
(When the sun sulks so do I)

Transit umbra; lux permanent
(The shadow passes: light is permanent)

I live in the present, a past I recall,
But my future depends on the strength of the wall

Thou by the dial's shady stealth may know
Time's thievish progress to eternity

-Shakespeare

PEACE IN THE GARDEN

Cooled by the shade of the cedar, refreshed by the contents of the amber glass in which ice tinkled so musically when he lifted it to his lips, the Hon. Galahad... had achieved a Nirvana-like repose. Storms may be raging elsewhere in the grounds of Blandings Castle, but there on the lawn there was a peace - the perfect unruffled peace which in this world seems to come only to those who have done nothing whatever to deserve it.

-P.G. Woodhouse

BEDDING PLANTS

This is a conveniently comprehensive term for the tender plants that are put out for the summer. To these plants a small portion of my garden, well sheltered within enclosing walls and yet open to full sunshine, is devoted, so that the little place is in some kind of beauty from the end of July to the last days in September. There has been so strong a revulsion in garden practice since the days when the bedding out of tender plants in stiff and not very intelligent ways absorbed the entire horticultural energy of owners of gardens that many people have conceived a dislike to the plants themselves. It is a common thing for friends to express surprise at seeing scarlet Geraniums, yellow Calceolaria and blue Lobelia in my garden, forgetting that it was not the fault of the plants that they were misused or employed in dull or even stupid ways.

-Gertrude Jekyll

Perhaps one of the most glorious, though to our
eyes, common, spectacles in the world, is the
first bursting into foliage of the leafless tree.
-Charles Darwin

JUNE

14

15

16

1848-Annual Horticultural Exhibition at Chiswick ruined by storms and heavy rain.

1993-First day of the BBC *Gardeners' World* live show, N.E.C., Birmingham.

17

18

19

20

1993-Close of the BBC *Gardeners' World* live show.

THOUGHTS IN A GARDEN

What wondrous life is this I lead
Ripe apples drop about my head;
The luscious clusters of the vine
Upon my mouth do crush their wine;
The nectarine and curious peach
Into my hands themselves do reach;
Stumbling on melons, as I pass,
Ensnared with flowers, I fall on grass.

-Andrew Marvell

Too quick despairer, wherefore wilt thou go?
Soon will the high Midsummer pomps come on,
Soon will the musk carnations break and swell,
Soon shall we have gold-dusted snapdragon,
Sweet-William with his homely cottage-smell,
And stocks in fragrant blow;
Roses that down the alleys shine afar,
And open, jasmine-muffled lattices,
And groups under the dreaming garden-trees,
And the full moon, and the white evening-star.

-Matthew Arnold

BELL-SHAPED FLOWERS

Flowers that are bell-shaped, with various patterns and colours, look attractive, but they also fulfil a practical role by attracting bees and moths. During rain, the bell hangs downward and protects the pollen of the flower. Bell-shaped flowers include:

❀ Canterbury Bell
❀ Harebell
❀ Bluebell
❀ Columbine
❀ Convolvulus
❀ Fuchsia
❀ Martagon Lily
❀ Anemone blanda
❀ Gentian
❀ White Fritillary
❀ Snake's Head Fritillary

21

22

23

24

25

26

27

1552-A man and woman were pilloried at Cheapside, London for selling short weight in fruit and vegetables in the market.

FORT PUTS THE CASE FOR THE BETTER BARROW

Wheelbarrows is an area where one could be forgiven for thinking that precious little real product development has taken place for many years. The market is flooded with "Me-Too" products, and discerning users will agree that most of them do not deliver a particularly useful performance or reasonable life-span to the consumer.

FORT has excited gardeners everywhere by going a radically different route. Founded in 1951, **FORT** maintains a heavy investment programme in new technology and new product development - a very successful effort resulting in several unique design features which offer the user a string of outstanding benefits:

POLYPROPYLENE TRAYS - lightweight, virtually indestructible, will never crack, chip, buckle, rust, fade or go brittle.

ONE-PIECE FRAMES, i.e. a single length of tubing wrought into shape - with fusion-welded cross members and not a bolt hole in sight, i.e. the frame is sealed from moisture, and rust will not start inside where you cannot see it or keep it in check.

TOP QUALITY WHEELS - FORT barrows roll on the largest wheels in the business - 16" x 4" (400 x 100mm), and are the only barrows to feature steel roller bearings. The large-size tyres allow the user to negotiate kerbs, ditches or gravelled areas in comfort - and the bearings guarantee the smoothest possible rolling performance for years and years.

These features apply to various of our most popular products. The *FK90 Easyrider* retails at well under £60 and has become the most popular barrow in its price bracket. Placing "Best Buy" in the "Gardening from Which" wheelbarrow test programme did not hurt its reputation either...

FORT has now launched a product to compete in the £30-£40 price bracket where so many products are hopelessly under-engineered and inadequate for meeting the expectations of modern consumers: The new *Weekender* barrow retails at under £40 but offers the user a truly remarkable specification at only a few Pounds more than many inferior products:

SEAMLESS PRESSED GALVANIZED TRAY - No joints, no rivets - with double-rolled edges for both safety and strength: It is not possible to reach a sharp edge with your fingers, and the edge will not buckle as do single-skin or wire-rolled edges.

ONE PIECE-FRAME - similar in concept to the frame on the *FK90 Easyrider*.

16" x 4" PNEUMATIC TYRE - 2-Ply, with a tube to allow DIY puncture repairs, and shockproof Polypropylene wheel rim complete with pre-lubricated needle bearings.

The *Weekender* sets new standards in its medium price range - just as decisively as the *Easyrider* did at the "Premium" end of the market when that was introduced... and it is not surprising that both are firm favourites with gardeners throughout the country.

Other **FORT** barrows include the *Evergreen* - which won a DIY New product of the Year Award in 1992 - and the *Jumbo* and *Mammoth* super-barrows for the estate and agricultural user. Whatever one's application or budget, **FORT** has a barrow guaranteed to suit the job, each of them probably the Best of Its Kind.

 Interval Systems

THE GARDENER

The gardener does not love to talk,
He makes me keep the gravel walk;
And when he puts his tools away
He locks the door and takes the key.

Away behind the currant row
Where no one else but cook may go,
Far in the plots, I see him dig,
Old and serious, brown and big.

He digs the flowers, green, red and blue,
Nor wishes to be spoken to.
He digs the flowers and cuts the hay,
And never seems to want to play.

Silly gardener! Summer goes,
And winter comes with pinching toes,
When in the garden bare and brown
You must lay your barrow down.

Well now, and while the summer stays,
To profit by these garden days,
O how much wiser you would be
To play at Indian wars with me!

-Robert Louis Stevenson

BORDEAUX AND BURGUNDY MIXTURES FOR FUNGICIDAL USE
(Much safer simply to drink the wine!)

The value of Bordeaux Mixture as a fungicide was discovered accidentally. It was the practice of the French vineyards to spray the vines by the side of the roads with this mixture to discourage pilfering and in about 1882 it was noticed that the sprayed plants developed less Mildew than the rest. This observation led to the use of the spray as a control for that disease and its use was extended to control Potato blight and Apple scab.

To make Bordeaux Mixture, prepare two stock solutions, one of copper sulphate dissolved at the rate of 1lb per gallon of water in a wooden or enamelled vessel; one of 1lb quicklime per gallon of water, slaked by the gradual addition of the water. To make up the mixture to a required strength, add the lime solution to water, stir well and then add the copper sulphate solution, stirring thoroughly.

Burgundy Mixture is considered a stronger fungicide than Bordeaux Mixture, and may be used in its place, especially to control rusts, and leaf curl disease of Peaches and Nectarines. The lime content is replaced by washing soda, using $1^3/_4$lb washing soda in place of 1lb lime. The copper sulphate solution is diluted before adding the washing soda solution, otherwise the method of making Burgundy Mixture is the same as for Bordeaux Mixture. A standard solution is one part copper sulphate solution, 1 part washing soda solution, 12 parts of water. Use within 24-36 hours.

- The Popular Encyclopaedia of Gardening,
c. 1942

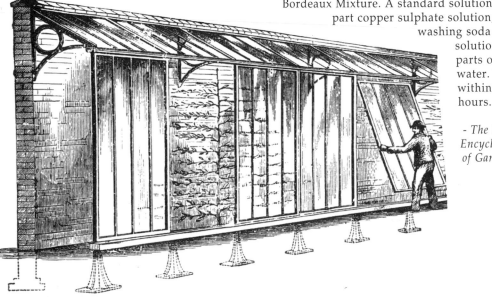

Lord Finchley tried to mend the Electric Light
Himself. It struck him dead; and serve him right!
It is the business of the wealthy man
To give employment to the artisan.

-Hilaire Belloc

28

29

30

1923-Suttons Seeds announces the largest-ever consignment of seeds despatched to New Zealand.

1

2

3

4

1958-Publication of the first issue of *Garden News*. The editorial stated: "This is, as far as we know, the world's first newspaper to be published weekly for gardeners."

Of the many things that should be thought of in the making of a garden to live in, this of fragrance is one of the first.

-Robinson

FRAGRANT COTTAGE FLOWERS

Apart from the groups of plants in which all, or nearly all, are fragrant, as in Roses, the annual and biennial flowers of our gardens are rich in fragrance - Stocks, Mignonette, Sweet Peas, Sweet Sultan, Wallflowers, double Rockets, Sweet Scabious, and many others. These, among the most easily raised of plants, may be enjoyed by the poorest cottage gardeners.

-Robinson

Music, when soft voices die,
Vibrates in the memory -
Odours, when sweet violets sicken,
Live within the sense they quicken.

Rose leaves, when the rose is dead,
Are heaped for the beloved's bed;
And so thy thoughts, when thou art gone,
Love itself shall slumber on.

-Percy Bysshe Shelley

LACED PINKS

Laced Pinks are characterised by double flowers and smoothly laid petals. The lacing colour should form a well marked eye in the centre of the flower, from which a narrow even band of colour should extend around the petal, leaving a clear patch of the ground colour in the centre of the petal. Those flowers in which the band of ground colour is equal in width to the lacing colour are deemed very desirable.

Varieties of Laced Pinks include:

* Dad's Favourite
* London Glow
* London Superb
* London Girl
* London Lady
* Murray's Laced Pink

- The Popular Encyclopaedia of Gardening, c. 1942

FRANCIS BACON'S CHOICE OF MOST SWEETLY SCENTED PLANTS

* Violet - especially the white-double violet
* Musk Rose
* Strawberry leaves drying
* Sweetbriar
* Wallflowers
* Pinks and Gilly-flowers
* Flowers of the Lime Tree
* Honeysuckle
* Burnet
* Wild thyme
* Water-Mints

NIGHT-SCENTED STOCK

This hardy annual (Matthiola bicornis) grows about 12in. in height, has rather splendid stems, and bears small, purplish-white flowers which are inconspicuous by day but open in the evening and then give off a delicious perfume. To obtain the full benefit of their fragrance, it is usual to grow them near the house so that the air, scented by their fragrance, is wafted through the open windows. As they are rather drab-looking by day, it is a good plan to mix an equal quantity of seeds of Virginia Stock (Malcolmia maritima) with them when sowing, to ensure colour by day.

I hesitate not a moment to prefer the plant of a fine carnation to a gold watch set with diamonds.

-William Cobbett

5

6

1785-Birth date of Joseph Hooker, botanist and plant explorer. Hooker was a friend of Charles Darwin and went on plant hunting expeditions to New Zealand, Morocco, India, Tasmania and other countries.

7

8

9

10

11

THE USEFULNESS OF WATTLE HURDLES, AND HOW TO KNOCK THEM UP

For obtaining protection against winds there is nothing better than a line of hurdles, whether of wood or iron it matters little, with brushwood, gorse, or even light faggot wood, interlaced vertically between the horizontal bars. This affords a rough but very effective shelter, and, if no hurdles are at command, it is easy enough to knock up a few frames of rough wood for the purpose by nailing to three or more uprights, according to the length, transverse bars, at a distance apart ranging from 6 inches to 9 inches, or thereabouts. Such hurdles are most useful in breaking the force and mitigating the rigour of a cold and boisterous wind.

*-The Beeton Book of
Garden Management*

THE MOST EFFICIENT EARWIG TRAP

Earwigs hide away as soon as they are disturbed, plunging into the flowers of dahlias, roses, carnations and others. A trap recommended as highly efficient was made from a wooden or metal box with a hole in the top

containing a funnel-shaped glass. The earwigs enter down the glass and are trapped inside. It was then recommended that boiling water should be poured on them to seal their fate.

TO A SQUIRREL

Come play with me;
Why should you run
Through the shaking tree
As though I'd a gun
To strike you dead?
When all I would do
Is to scratch your head
And let you go.

-W.B. Yeats

SOME ADVICE ON HANGING BASKETS

Another feature in "window gardening" is the introduction of suspended baskets, usually made of wire, for the purpose of displaying to advantage the beautiful habit of trailing plants. These should be potted in ordinary flower pots and surrounded with moss in the basket, the latter being made to hook on to a support in the ceiling, so that it may be temporarily removed when the plant requires water. In planting a basket, if it is to be filled with ordinary soft-wooded flowering plants, that is, ivy-leaf geraniums, verbenas, petunias etc., the soil ought to be two-thirds loam to one of very rotten dung or leaf mould, and a little sand; if planted with ferns or hard-wooded plants the soil should be one half turfy loam and one half peat, using rather more sand than for the free-growing plants.

To those who are not acquainted with soils, it may be worthwhile to observe that good loam is of a yellowish hue, and feels soft and silky to the touch; it is usually the top spit of meadow land, while peat is obtained in places where heath grows wild.

*-The Beeton Book of
Garden Management*

I like spiders and I like nettles because they are hated.

-Victor Hugo

JULY

12

13

14

15

1838-Birth of William Robinson, known as the "Father of the English Flower Garden" in County Down, Northern Ireland. His famous garden was at Gravetye Manor in Sussex.

16

17

18

And in the warm hedge grew lush eglantine,
Green cowbind and the moonlight-coloured may,
And cherry-blossoms, and white cups, whose wine
Was the bright dew, yet drained not by the day;
And wild roses, and ivy serpentine,
With its dark buds and leaves, wandering astray;
And flowers azure, black, and streaked with gold,
Fairer than any wakened eyes behold.

-Percy Bysshe Shelley

I have heard the pigeons of the Seven Woods
Make their faint thunder, and the garden bees
Hum in the lime-tree flowers; and put away
The unavailing outcries and the old bitterness
That empty the heart.

-W.B. Yeats, *In The Seven Woods*

CRAB APPLE.

PYRUS MALUS.

DOWNY LEAVED ROSE.

ROSA TOMENTOSA

COMMON DOG ROSE.

BLACKTHORN or SLOE.

PRUNUS SPINOSA.

ROSA CANINA.

THE DELICACY OF SHAPE AND COLOUR OF THE "WILD" ROSES OF THE HEDGEROW IS PERFECT FOR COTTAGE GARDENS

A garden haunted by the nightingale's
Long trills and gushing ecstasies of song.
-Thomas Campbell

JULY

19

20

1993 Flower Show at the R.H.S. Halls, Westminster featuring a Summer Fruit and Vegetable Competition.

21

22

23

24

25

1622-Founding of Oxford Botanic Garden.

SUNDAY SUPPLEMENT GARDENS

Some people make a garden because it is a fashionable thing to do. They have themselves photographed for society magazines and Sunday supplements, in their gardens (made by their host of gardeners), wearing smart clothes and all the jewelled panoply of Dives. I have a notion that when such pictures are taken all the little birds in the tree-tops have a difficult time to prevent themselves from bursting with laughter.

-Richardson Wright, 1922

After sitting long enough to admire every article of furniture in the room, from the sideboard to the fender, to give an account of their journey, and of all that had happened in London, Mr. Collins invited them to take a stroll in the garden, which was large and well laid out, and to the cultivation of which he attended himself. To work in his garden was one of his most respectable pleasures.

-Jane Austen, *Pride and Prejudice*

Try to keep a garden beautiful to yourself alone and see what happens - the neighbour, hurrying to catch his train of mornings, will stop to snatch a glint of joy from the iris purpling by your doorstep. The motorist will throw on brakes and back downhill just to see those Oriental poppies massed against the wall. Nature is always on the side of the public. Build your wall never so high but her winds will carry the seeds of that choice variety you reserved for yourself to a dozen different dooryards and open fields, where they will blossom next season. Plant your hedgerow never so thick but a vine will stretch forth a friendly finger through it. Lock the gate never so tight but the Zephyrs will waft odors of rose and hyacinth and mignonette to every passer-by.

-Richardson Wright, 1922

ALICE TALKS TO THE FLOWERS

"How is it you can talk so nicely?" Alice said... "I've been in many gardens before, but none of the flowers could talk."

"Put your hand down and feel the ground", said the Tiger-lily. "Then you'll know why."

Alice did so. "It's very hard," she said; "but I don't see what that has to do with it."

"In most gardens," the Tiger-lily said, "they make the beds too soft - so that the flowers are always asleep."

This sounded a very good reason, and Alice was quite pleased to know it. "I never thought of that before!" she said.

"It's my opinion that you never think <u>at all</u>," the Rose said, in a rather severe tone.

-Lewis Carroll, *Through the Looking Glass*

Oh, what a pity is it
That he had not so trimm'd and dress'd his land,
As we this garden!

-Shakespeare

JULY/AUGUST

26

1894-The *Gardener's Chronicle* reported a boom in the public taste for pot plants and cut flowers made into posies, coronets, fans and body sprays.

27

28

29

30

31

1

THE JOY OF TERRACOTTA FROM Olive Tree

ONE OF THE OLDEST MATERIALS

Terracotta is one of the oldest materials known to man and clay pots have been in use ever since the early Nile fishermen, several thousand years ago, found that their dry nets full of clay and mud actually held water. Terracotta vases and urns have been in use in gardens since Roman Times and their use became popular in Europe in the 17th and 18th centuries. The Great Exhibition of London in 1851 had over 20 different manufacturers of clay pottery showing their wares, and the Victorians used pots both in their gardens and conservatories.

THE TERRACOTTA REVIVAL

In this century the advent of plastic all but killed off clay in the immediate post war period, but the last ten years or so have seen a great terracotta revival in this country. Olive Tree started promoting their wide range of pottery in the 1970s, travelling the world in search of the best design and quality. They were also the first national distributor in this country to reassure the public with a Frost Guarantee. As a natural material, terracotta appeals strongly to all those who want to surround themselves with beautiful objects that are at the same time not wasting the earth's resources.

ADVANTAGES FOR THE GARDENER

Olive Tree terracotta, of course, has many distinct advantages for the gardener. The porosity of the clay helps with keeping the roots at an even temperature and also improves the flow of oxygen. It also means that it is difficult to over-water a plant in a clay pot, and that excess fertilisers and chemicals may leach out through the wall of the pot. The weight of a clay pot is an important factor in windy conditions and with particularly tall plants.

USEFUL HINTS WHEN PLANTING UP POTS

There are a few useful hints to bear in mind when planting up your Olive Tree pots. Soak the pot in water before planting, as otherwise when you first water all the moisture will be absorbed by the pot rather than going into the soil. Use plenty of crock in the bottom of the pot for better drainage and to ensure that the drainage hole itself does not get blocked by the roots. Using Olive Tree pot feet will keep the pot off the ground, which not only helps to keep pests out but helps with the drainage as well.

The joy of Olive Tree terracotta is that there are so many designs and shapes to choose from. Groups of pots together on a patio or terrace look wonderful. There are window boxes and bulb bowls and strategically placed pots can work wonders in a flower bed to fill seasonal gaps or to add a bit of height. One other great advantage is being able to move pots around to change the character and shape of your garden at will.

MARKET LEADERS

Olive Tree Trading are the market leaders in the distribution of terracotta in this country. They have over 500 different products in their range which covers not only terracotta but also glazed pottery and ceramics from all over the world. Their outdoor products are all covered by a Ten Year Replacement Guarantee in case of frost damage and their products are to be found in most leading garden centres throughout the United Kingdom.

Olive Tree Terracotta

Guaranteed frost resistant, look for the label

Available from leading Garden Centres

DeRoMa

FASCINATING FACTS ABOUT THE EARTHWORM

There are 25 species of earthworm native to Britain.

Worms love soil with high organic content.

They swallow the soil and digest decaying plant and animal matter.

Worms have no head, nor eyes, and only a simple brain. They have no lungs, and absorb oxygen through their skin.

Worms usually live in the top nine inches of the soil, but go much deeper in extremely cold or dry conditions.

If it is cut, a worm can grow a new end, but separate halves cannot grow back together.

Worms constantly tunnel through soil, bringing air and drainage channels to benefit the roots of plants.

GARDEN BUTTERFLIES

Large White

Wall Brown

Small White

Peacock

Painted Lady

Ringlet

Green-Veined White

Small Tortoiseshell

Brimstone

Red Admiral

Comma

Small Copper

Holly Blue

Orange-Tip

Hedge Brown

SOME TYPES OF GARDEN MOTH

Privet Hawkmoth	Popular Hawkmoth
Eyed Hawkmoth	Hummingbird Hawkmoth
Buff-Tip	Lackey Moth
White Ermine	Buff Ermine
Goldtail Moth	Vapourer Moth
Grey Dagger	Large Yellow Underwing
Cabbage Moth	Dot Moth
Heart-and Dart Moth	Turnip Moth
Setaceous Hebrew Character	Clay Wainscot
Grey Dagger Moth	Old Lady
Mouse Moth	Angle Shades
Silver-Y Moth	Burnished Brass
Herald Moth	Beaded Chestnut
Swallow-Tailed	Brimstone Moth
Magpie Moth	Spinach Moth
Snout Moth	Garden Carpet
Yellow Shell	Pug Moths
Winter Moth	Mottled Umber
Ghost Swift Moth	Common Swift
Currant Clearwing	White Plume
Small Magpie	Mother-of-Pearl
Gold Fringe Moth	Garden Pebble
Small Ermine	Codlin Moth

-The Natural History of the Garden, Michael Chinery

And seeing the snail, which everywhere doth roam,
Carrying his own house, still is at home,
Follow (for he is easy paced) this snail,
Be thine own palace, or the world's thy gaol.

-John Donne

AUGUST

2

1712-The *Spectator* reported on a boat journey on the River Thames with traders from Covent Garden Market. The Market was then well established and many deliveries were made by boat, including melons and apricots.

3

4

1900-Birth date of H.M. Queen Elizabeth the Queen Mother, holder of the Victoria Medal of Horticulture and Patron of the Garden Society. Her own most famous garden is at Castle May in Scotland.

5

6

7

1882-Joseph Rochford set up his own nursery at Waltham Cross, Hertfordshire.

8

*CURLED OR
DOUBLE CHERVIL*

HERBAL REMEDIES THAT HAVE CONTINUED IN USE FOR CENTURIES

Sowbread and watercress to make hair grow

Elder rob for colds

Elder ointment for chapped hands and chilblains

Dandelion tea for sluggish livers

Infusion of dandelion for inflamed eyes

Apple water for feverish colds

An infusion of Borage for coughs

Bruised Caraway seeds pounded with breadcrumbs for earache

Infusion of Lesser Celandine for piles

Boiled nettle-leaves for asthma

Fresh Sage leaves to whiten teeth

Sweetened Thyme tea for whooping-cough

DRYING AND STORING HERBS

In the 16th century, herb gardens were usually divided into two parts - one for the pot herbs and the other for the physic herbs. Thomas Hyll advised that herbs should be picked and dried by hanging them up "in some Garrette or open room and high, being sweet and dry through the Sun's dayly shining on the place at noon." He said that dried herbs were best kept in leather bags or in boxes made of wood from the Box tree, to avoid losing their proper moisture.

THE OUTLANDISH ROSE

Gerard describes the "Garden Mallow called 'Hollyhocke' "as a plant with a tall, straight stem, "whereon do grow upon slender footstalks single floures, not much unlike to the wild Mallow, but greater, consisting only of five leaves, sometimes white or red, now and then of a deep purple colour, varying diversely as Nature list to play with it: in their places groweth up a round knop like a little cake, compact or made up of a multitude of flat seeds like little cheeses. The root is long, white, tough, easily bowed, and groweth deep in the ground.

*HOLLYHOCK
(Althæa rosea)*

These Hollihockes are sowne in gardens, almost everywhere, and are in vaine sought elsewhere. The second yeere after they are sowne they bring forth their floures in July and August. When the seed is ripe the root remaineth and sendeth forth new stalkes, leaves and floures, many years after.

The Hollihocke is called of divers, Rosa ultra-marina, or outlandish Rose."

A weed is no more than a flower in disguise,
Which is seen through at once, if love give a man
eyes.

-J.R. Lowell

9

10

1993-Flower Show at the R.H.S. Halls, Westminster featuring a
Gladiolus and Ornamental Plant Competition.

11

12

13

14

15

1878-International Congress of Botany and
Horticulture held in Paris.

LONDON VEGETABLE GARDENS, 1792

There are about five thousand acres within twelve miles of the metropolis constantly cultivated for the supply of the London markets with garden vegetables, exclusive of about eight hundred acres cropped with fruit of various kinds, and about 1,700 acres cultivated for potatoes. The culture is carried on most extensively in the parishes of Camberwell and Deptford St. Paul's, by persons who are called farming gardeners. Their method is to manure their land to the highest pitch of cultivation for garden crops, both for the market and for cattle, after a succession of which they refresh it by sowing it with corn.

In the parish of Fulham the cultivation of gardens for the market is carried on to a greater extent than any other in the kingdom. The cultivation of asparagus is carried in Deptford St. Paul's, Chiswick, Battersea, and Mortlake. Deptford is famous also for the culture of onions for seed.

The average rent of garden-ground in most of the parishes near London is now £4 per acre.

-Lysons

SOME 19TH CENTURY VEGETABLES

Peas - *some 18 varieties, including Sugar Peas*

Broad Beans - *10 varieties were grown*

Kidney Beans

Scarlet Runner Beans

Cabbage - *numerous varieties*

Brussel Sprouts - *grown from seed obtained from Brussels, as home stock was considered inferior*

Borecole - *some 14 varieties*

Beetroot - *used in salads and also dried and ground to mix with coffee, as an economy*

Parsnip - *in Northern Ireland roots were brewed with hops*

Scorzorena - *a native of southern Europe*

Salsify

Skirrets - *a native of China*

Spinach

White Beet

Orach (Good King Henry)

Sorrel

New Zealand Spinach

Onions

Leeks

Chives

Garlic

Shallots

Asparagus

Seakale

Globe Artichokes - *French Conical, Globe and Dwarf Globe were all popular*

16

1716-Baptism of Lancelote (later "Capability Brown") in Northumberland. Brown became probably the most famous landscape gardener ever.

17

1661-Grand opening of Vaux-le-Vicomte, the first garden created by le Nôtre.

1878-*Tulipa Kolpakowskiana* launched in Britain. (Discovered in Turkestan by Albert Regel).

18

1855-Publication of new, enlarged edition of Dr. Lindley's *Theory and Practice of Horticulture*.

19

20

21

22

A GREAT INTEREST IN CUCUMBERS

The best contested classes at the 1866 Exhibition were for cucumbers. Long before that time interest in this vegetable was very great, and special societies existed for the holding of competitions among growers. The rule laid down was that a cucumber "should be a foot long, straight, of even thickness, with a flower still fresh upon its point; let it, moreover, be short-necked, firm, brittle, and a free bearer. If of the old, prickly race,

bloom should be insisted on, but as cucumbers of the Smyrna and Turkish breed have no bloom, and as they are among the best for table, to require bloom as a sine qua non would be to exclude some of the most useful sorts of cultivation." The old method was to grow the plants on dung hot-beds, allowing the shoots to trail on the surface. A Mr. Mills, about 1842, brought out Mills's Improved Cucumber Pit, stated to be capable of furnishing a supply of fruits every month of the year, which was considered a remarkable achievement.

-G.F. Tinley, *The Horticultural Record*

A CONTEMPLATION OF "NEW VEGETABLES" IN 1914

No new vegetable of first-rate importance has been added to our gardens during recent years. Maize or corn is cultivated in warm districts for its succulent heads, but it needs a very favourable season to bring it to maturity. This vegetable is consumed largely in America, and we owe its introduction to that source. The aubergine and other egg plants are valued by some as vegetables, but their cultivation is very limited. The Chinese artichoke, Stachys tuberifera, makes a nice dish in winter and deserves a more extended cultivation in this country. Capsicums are used for saladings and other purpose, but their chief value is a decorative one. New Zealand Spinach is a great acquisition, the crop succeeding excellently in the hottest weather, when ordinary spinach fails. Much has been written in the gardening Press lately of the value of the Soy bean, which is grown like the kidney bean, and is very popular as a vegetable in America.

AUGUST

23

24

25

26

27

28

29

1673-The Apothecaries' Company first signed the lease on the Chelsea Physic Garden, at Cheyne Walk in London.

TUFF-LINK - MANUFACTURERS OF TRELLIS AND DECORATIVE FENCING

THE FIRST "MAINTENANCE FREE" TRELLIS - TRELLEX

TUFF-LINK is a unique family-owned manufacturing company located in the north of England near the lovely Ribble Valley and born out of a singular opportunity to manufacture nylon and plastic chains. The market quickly developed into gardening and as TUFF-LINK expanded the first plastic trellisworks evolved. Previously, almost all trellis had been made of wood and the new material, whilst retaining the perceived warmth of wood and giving kind and firm support, was celebrated for being longer lasting and maintenance free. Later, fine plastic coated metal trellis was added to the range, and, whilst being strictly alert to reforestation, wooden trellis is now also manufactured under the TUFF-LINK banner.

A ROMANTIC GARDEN FEATURE

Trellis is the most romantic of all garden features. Its versatility is endless. Whilst being comfortable on the humblest abode it has the superb elegance required for the palaces of kings. Named first by the French, they also developed the exciting illusionary trelliage which is so often seen in garden rooms and conservatories of the Victorian era. The Victorians positively wallowed in trellis structures, and pictures of very elaborate affairs have been passed down for our entertainment. Arbours and archways, pergolas and pillars, the latter joined by chains of roses, still feature in gardens of the late 20th century. Today we have modified our tastes and our gardens, due to the fact that most of us do not employ resident gardeners! Now gardeners are usually the residents and so need easy maintenance.

A GREATER CHOICE

Trellis will screen, fence, support or frame. The greater variety of materials used makes for even greater choice. Traditional wooden trellises are pre-treated with preservatives where necessary. Larger structures are packed flat. Most products have fittings and instructions for easy assembly.

A PLACE FOR RELAXATION

Gardens are a place for relaxation, and to this end TUFF-LINK have introduced beautiful NEW shades of plastic TRELLEX which compliment the natural stonework and the exciting brickwork colours of new and old masonry. Meranti, a warm brown mahogany is new and the range of architectural trellises for picturesque wall effects, so beneficial in town gardens and small areas, is being extended.

What could be more rewarding than a good natured framework for the environment in which we enjoy our relaxation?

"and add to these retired leisure that in trim gardens takes his pleasure"
-Milton, L'Allegro

THE STRONGEST NAME
IN TRELLIS

We are manufacturers of the worlds leading plastic and timber trellis.

The durable plastic TRELLEX offers a multichoice of colour finishes, including white, green, brown, terracotta, sandstone and limestone.

The timber ranges offer a similar variety of styles including traditional, fan and square mesh trellis, beautifully finished from a variety of woods.

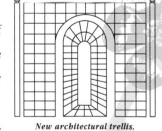

New architectural trellis.
(Trelliage Decoratif)

Expanding or rigid, discreet or heavy duty plant pot or architectural, there is a Tuff-Link trellis to suit your needs and enhance your gardening.

Available from most garden centres and nurseries, leading D.I.Y. stores and other independent garden outlets. For your full colour brochure telephone: 0282 779721.

TUFF-LINK LTD., TUFF-LINK HOUSE, STATION ROAD, PADIHAM, LANCASHIRE, BB12 7AR
TELEPHONE: 0282 779721   FACSIMILE: 0282 778489

THE EDUCATION OF YOUNG GARDENERS, 1912

As regards school gardens, they are still largely experimental, and everything depends on the master. If he is a born gardener he will cultivate habits of method, develop habits of tidiness in tools and culture, and sometimes, perhaps, answer satisfactorily the questions of lads and girls.

With regard to secondary schools the same remarks apply... No attempt should be made at special technical instruction in horticulture. The development of the English instinct for gardening is a national asset, for the health of our people depends on fresh supplies of fruit and vegetables from gardens and allotments.

One thing must be more encouraged, and that is the making of vegetable soups and the cooking of vegetables. Much pastry-making instruction could be eliminated. Badly made soup is better than indigestible pastry.

*-The Rev. J. Bernard Hall,
Secretary to the North of
England Horticultural Society*

It may interest you to know about the progress of Horticulture. I am sorry to say I am a very old man. When I was a boy there were only two flower shops in London - one at one end of Covent Garden and the other at the other end. One was that of Mrs. Bick and the other of that of Mrs. Johnson, and this latter shop still exists. A little later another flower-shop was opened in London - Harding's - The gardener of my grandmother - Mr. Mills - retired and went to Ealing, and he was the first to raise roses of a good class. He had a contract with Harding's to supply roses for which he received £300 a year, and he was not allowed to sell roses to anyone else. Now you can buy roses anywhere in London better than you could get then.

-Mr. Leopold de Rothschild, 1912

THE SECURITY OF A CHILDHOOD GARDEN

I could gain my liberty at any moment by means of an easy climb over a gate, a wall, or a little sloping roof, but as soon as I landed back on the gravel of our own garden, illusion and faith returned to me. For as soon as she asked me: "Where have you come from?" and frowned the ritual frown, my mother would resume her placid, radiant garden-face, so much more beautiful than her anxious indoor-face. And merely because she held sway there and watched over it all, the walls grew higher, the enclosures which I had so easily traversed by jumping from wall to wall and branch to branch, became unknown lands, and I found myself once more among the familiar wonders.

-Colette,
Sido

COVENT GARDEN MARKET: CENTRAL AVENUE, C.1876

I am not yet born; provide me

With water to dandle me, grass to grow for me, trees to talk to me, sky to sing to me, birds and a white light in the back of my mind to guide me.

-Louis Macneice, *Prayer Before Birth*

30

31

1

1993-National Dahlia Society Show, R.H.S. New Hall, Westminster.

2

1914-Cancellation of Dahlia Conference, White City, due to requisition of building for military purposes.

3

4

5

THE PRICE OF A TULIP

In the 1630s Holland was gripped by a mania for tulips and bulbs changed hands at massive prices. An author of the day recorded that one person was so anxious to posses a single root of a rare species called the *Viceroy* that he paid for it with all the following goods:

- Two lasts of wheat
- Four lasts of rye
- Four fat oxen
- Eight fat swine
- Twelve fat sheep
- Two hogsheads of wine
- Four tuns of beer
- Two tuns of butter
- One thousand 1lbs of cheese
- A complete bed
- A suit of clothes
- A silver drinking cup

In England it was said that a tulip could produce more money than an oak, and that if a black tulip could be found, its price would equal that of a dozen acres of standing corn. In 1800, a common price was fifteen guineas for a single bulb and in 1835 a bulb of the species called the Miss Fanny Kemble was sold by public auction for seventy five pounds.

- Charles Mackay,
Memoirs of Extraordinary Popular Delusions

Tulipa species recommended by Jane Loudon included T. oculus-solis, T. cornuta, T. sylvestris, T. suaveolens, T. montana, T. capensis and T. biflora.

1. *Tulipa oculus solis.* 2. *Tulipa cornuta.* 3. *Tulipa sylvestris.* 4. *Tulipa Gesneriana.*
5. *Tulipa suaveolens.* 6. *Tulipa montana.* 7. *Tulipa capensis.* 8. *Tulipa biflora.*

What is this Toolip? A well-complexion'd stink,
an ill favour wrapt up in pleasant colours.
                                    -Thomas Fuller

SEPTEMBER

6

7

8

9

1914-First annual exhibition of the London Gardens Association,
Vincent Square, London.

10

11

12

The Gentian is another of those desirable, early and rare old plants of great beauty. Nothing can excel the beauty of a few small beds of this lovely tribe. Acaulis is stemless, as the name indicates. It·is a plant bearing a lovely blue trumpet flower as far as stature goes, and in consequence the flower becomes most conspicuous. In some localities this plant is said to be difficult to grow, and more difficult to induce into flower; but if it is planted in a somewhat shady aspect, in soil composed of good friable loam, a little peat, and some road sand, with a little old lime rubbish, sifted and well mixed with the rest, draining the bed, it will succeed well.

HOW TO PRODUCE BEAUTIFUL BLUENESS IN HYDRANGEAS

There is a particular sympathy among all lovers of flowers for blue. I suppose this happens in consequence of all flowers, whether species or genera, running principally upon every colour and shade but blue; but in the case of the hydrangea there is good cause for the want of blue, as there are no true blue species or varieties.

I know of a locality where lovely blue hydrangeas are naturally produced; that locality possesses a large amount of iron, tin, and mundic in the soil; and although peat, it will not grow heaths at all. The blue may be produced anywhere by first growing the hydrangea in peat, then supplying it with the necessary element; and this can be produced artificially by keeping tin and iron ore in the water with which the plants are watered; but I would advise those who wish to grow this plant to produce blue flowers to get some of the peat, so famous for producing it, from Dartmoor, where it constantly flowers blue.

-Samuel Wood,
Good Gardening,
1876

Bats flying in greater number herald fine weather for the hours of darkness.
-French proverb

13

1879-The lawn mower had become such an essential part of upper and middle-class homes and gardens that *Punch* published a cartoon about the disturbance caused by the gardener with his noisy machine.

14

15

16

17

1993-Great Autumn Show, Exhibition Halls, Harrogate (two days).

18

19

SWING WATER BARROW

MAKING A NEW LAWN
Preparing to Sow Seed:

The soil should be dug and levelled several weeks ahead of sowing. Good drainage is highly important, being essential to the welfare of the finer lawn grasses.

Fertilizing should be done about 2-3 weeks before sowing. A good general fertilizer is one of 4 parts by weight super-phosphate, 2 parts sulphate of ammonia, and 1 part sulphate of potash, at $1^1/_2$ to 2oz. per sq. yds.

The final preparation of the seed bed should be done a fortnight before sowing, raking to produce a fine tilth, and rolling lightly, when non-sticky and dryish, in two opposite directions, to give firmness. Then rake to provide the fine tilth ready for sowing.

Choice of Seed Mixture:

For fine lawns only two or three species of grass are necessary, chosen from bents and fescues. A good mixture for most soils in open situations is:

7 parts by weight Chewing's Fescue, and 3 parts New Zealand Browntop

or: 3 parts by weight Chewing's Fescue, 4 parts Creeping Red Fescue and 3 parts New Zealand Browntop

Lawns from Turf:

These are costly, but more quickly made. Good turf is expensive and not too common. Care should be paid to the species of grass present, rather than to the weeds. Old parkland turf is good. Sea-washed marsh or Cumberland turf needs good management to be satisfactory. Downland turf is useful. Experience suggests that turf from heaths and moorlands succeed best under garden conditions. Before laying, each turf should be inspected and any rosette weeds or coarse grasses pulled or pushed out.

Turfing should begin at one side or corner, and laying is done facing the prepared soil, the gardener standing or kneeling on a board to avoid indenting the newly laid turf. The turves are laid with joints alternating, like brickwork, but packed closely together.

Watering will be needed in dry weather, and if the turf is inclined to crack, top-dressings of sand and peat in equal proportions should be applied.

-The Popular Encyclopaedia of Gardening, c. 1942

GARDEN ENGINE

SEPTEMBER

20

21

22

23

24

25

1878-The International Potato Exhibition held at Crystal Palace.

26

SowEasy - *making gardening easier*

Gardening is a very traditional pastime but gardeners themselves are always experimenting. By nature they are forward looking, always planning the activities that lie ahead, whatever time of year, and garden product manufacturers are also concerned with new approaches to old problems, whether it be to increase yield and quality or to make gardening easier and safer.

EASIER GARDENING

The SowEasy Company have dedicated themselves to this task, marketing products that make gardening a little easier and more productive, whilst being sympathetic to our environment. Take our Jiffy products for example:- used for more than 20 years by Professional Gardeners worldwide. The range now includes recycled paper pots as well as the famous Jiffy 7. Jiffy 7s are supplied as small convenient sized pellets which when watered expand to become perfect small pots for planting seeds or starting off cuttings. Nothing could be easier and because they contain all the nutrients the growing plants need, they are not checked for transplanting.

KEEPING POT PLANTS MOIST

The Jiffy Aquamat, using the capillary system adopted by growers to keep pot plants moist, is the product to use when you go on holiday to keep your plants alive.

BAMBOO

Bamboo, which is easily grown in managed plantations is used for two of SowEasy's products. Jiffy sticks are natural and free from harmful chemicals. Our lawn rake, which has been a best-seller in the U.S.A. for 70 years, is also made from bamboo, a surprising material to use for a product that receives such hard wear. However, bamboo is very strong, flexible and to make the task of collecting garden debris and leaves easier, very light. A delight to use.

A FRENCH DESIGN

The design of our pot holders is French, and the range makes it easy to brighten balconies, windows, fences and walls with flowers and foliage throughout the year, just as they do on the continent.

Finally, there can be no easier way of sowing seeds than to use Seed Sticks, seeds on the end of degradable cardboard sticks. The system makes seeds very easy to handle and is ideal for handicapped gardeners and for children. Also an ideal fund raiser.

SowEasy will continue to bring interesting new products to the traditional garden scene.

Mankind will never look upon taking fruit in an orchard, or a garden, as felony, nor even as a serious trespass. Besides, there are such things as *boys*, and every considerate man will recollect, that he himself was once a boy... Resolve, therefore to share the produce of your garden with the whole neighbourhood; or, to keep it for your own use by a fence that they cannot get through, over, or under.

-William Cobbett

SEPARATED BY THE GARDEN FENCE

The first thing I did on my own account, when I came back, was to take a night-walk to Norwood and, like the subject of a venerable riddle of my childhood, to go 'round and round the house, without ever touching the house' thinking about Dora. I believe the theme of this incomprehensible conundrum was the moon. No matter what it was, I, the moon-struck slave of Dora, perambulated round and round the house and garden for two hours, looking through crevices in the palings, getting my chin by dint of violent exertion above the rusty nails on the top, blowing kisses at the lights in the windows, and romantically calling on the night, at intervals, to shield my Dora - I don't know exactly what from, I suppose from fire. Perhaps from mice, to which she had a great objection.

-Charles Dickens, *David Copperfield*

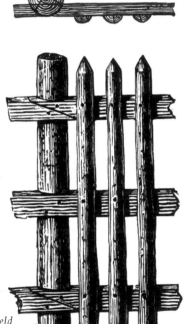

COPING TO WALLS, 1890

Coping to garden walls has been a "much-vexed" question, and probably many practical men retain their own system, without paying much attention to theories; for in gardening, a common-sense application of the means at hand, and taking everything at the right time is of more importance than the best-formed theory imperfectly carried out. It seems very well settled, however, that a stone coping projecting an inch or two over the wall on each side, is necessary for the protection of the wall from the effects of rain, and that, to that extent, the coping is useful in retarding the radiation of heat.

MAKING A RUSTIC FENCE, ARCH OR PERGOLA

The wood commonly used for rustic work is Larch, but Oak is preferable, having the virtue of longer life, although the initial cost is a little more. Rustic furniture is usually made from Oak; this is sometimes used with the bark on, but is better peeled, the wood in the latter case being varnished, with or without staining.

The tools required by a handyman for Rustic Work are few. A saw and hammer are enough for most purposes; for some of the more elaborate work a chisel and brace and bits are useful. There is also a type of saw known as a bow saw, having a thin blade kept in tension by twisted string, and capable of being twisted at an angle by the handle at each end. Such a saw will be found very handy where curved joints have to be cut, and for working green wood, where an ordinary carpenter's saw would become stuck by sap and resin. Easily made is a rustic fence with gate, the two gate posts being higher than the rest and 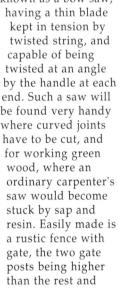 arched at the top. When erecting this type of work, measure out the pieces and cut the necessary joints, then put the uprights in the ground first, scraping the bottoms and giving a coat of gas tar. It is a good plan to bed each post on stones, and to ram in stones when filling the up the hole. From 18in. to 2ft. of the post should be below the soil, and tarring is extended a little way above, as decay takes place chiefly at ground level. After the uprights are firmly set, the cross bars are added; filling in with thin, latticed pieces is best left until the end.

Love thy neighbour but pull not down thy hedge.
-Anon

27

28

1855-The Government announces its intention to build a bridge
and footpath through St. James Park. Public outcry.

29

30

1

2

3

ON THE FIRST FLIGHT OF BEES

Hark! what is so gaily humming
In that little garden there?
Hark! what is so briskly whizzing
Through the still and silent air?

Friend, it is our bees - the darlings -
Now enlivened by the spring;
Yes, the winter is departed,
And once more they're on the wing.

Happy he, who winter's perils
All his stocks brings safely through;
Thank Him, of all good the Giver -
Faithful Watchman He, and true.

Of my own are none departed,
All as yet unhurt remain;
Though no longer rich in honey,
Yet is spring returned again!

Come, and let us view them nearer -
Enter by the garden gate; -
So stand still and watch their doings -
Light your pipe and patient wait.

See how busily they traverse
To their pasturage and back,
That they may toil unwearied
Save the commonwealth from wreck.

How they dart and how they hurtle
Through the genial balmy air!
To the mountains - to the meadows -
'Tis the scent attracts them there!

There they dexterously rifle
Nectar from each flower in bloom.
Toil they for our honey harvest,
For us fill the honey - room

-A Devonshire Bee-Keeper
(From the German of
Adalbert Braun)

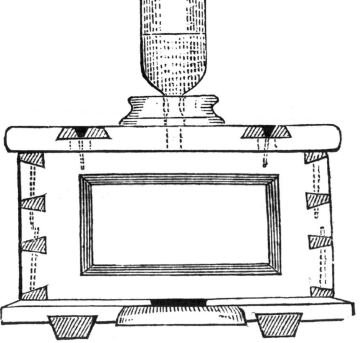

APPARATUS FOR UNITING BEES

"Try the bottle for your Ligurians applied in this fashion, through a block of wood with a bit of perforated zinc interposed. The neck of the bottle need not enter the hole in the top of the hive."

-From a letter to the *Journal of Horticulture and Cottage Gardener*, November 3rd, 1863

For fountains, they are a great beauty and refreshment; but pools mar all and make the garden unwholesome and full of flies and frogs.

-Francis Bacon, 1625

4

5

1993-Flower Show at the R.H.S. Halls, Westminster featuring Autumn Fruit and Vegetable Competition.

6

7

8

9

10

1908-The National Chrysanthemum Society finally succumbed to pressure to consider moving their shows to the R.H.S. Hall at Westminster.

GREENHOUSE FUMIGATION, 1914

Mr. Edwards' of Leeds patent cyaniding machine for fumigating the greenhouse: *a scoop trap containing cyanide and a tank containing water and sulphuric acid are installed in the greenhouse. A clockwork device is set and will start after a fifty second delay to empty the scoop into the tank, thus enabling the operator to escape the fumes.*

GREENHOUSE BOILERS

In Victorian times large greenhouses were heated by sometimes massive coal-fired boilers that circulated water around hundreds or even thousands of feet of pipes. The **CHALLENGE, VIADUCT** and **PYTHON** were all models in the range of Keith's Patent Boilers for greenhouses, awarded twenty prize medals at International Exhibitions at home and abroad. The **PYTHON** boiler had 1,000 sq. ft. of effective heating surface, $17^1/_2$ sq. ft. of fire-grate area, heated about 20,000 sq. ft. of 4in. pipe and claimed to be the Most Powerful and Complete Sectional "Special" Hot-water heating Boiler in the world. James Keith, heating engineer, was based in Holborn Viaduct, London.

SITTING IN THE GREENHOUSE, LISTENING TO THE BEES

My greenhouse is never so pleasant as when we are just upon the point of being turned out of it... I sit with all the windows and the door wide open, and am regaled with the scent of every flower, in a garden as full of flowers as I have known how to make it. We keep no bees, but if I lived in a hive, I should hardly hear more of their music. All the bees in the neighbourhood resort to a bed of mignonette opposite to the window, and pay me for the honey they get out of it with which a hum, though rather monotonous, is as agreeable to my ears as the whistling of my linnets.

-William Cowper

LIGHTING AND REGULATING THE BOILER

In the 1940s boilers like the **PYTHON** were still in use and an encyclopaedia gave the following daunting instructions:

To regulate the fire, so that it burns steadily throughout the night, the damper should be pushed in, leaving only about one inch exposed. The actual distance can only be determined by experiment.

In the morning the dampers should first be pulled out to allow the fumes to escape up the flue. The fire and ash doors are opened. The fire is stirred, the ashes and clinkers are raked out and the ashbox is cleared. Then sufficient fuel (coke or anthracite coal) is put on the fire to last until evening and when it is burning freely the dampers should be closed.

Like many of the upper class
He liked the sound of broken glass.
-Hilaire Belloc

OCTOBER

11

12

13

14

15

16

17

1920-Death of Reginald Farrer, great plant explorer and writer, in Upper Burma during a plant hunting expedition.

THE PROUD PRODUCER OF VEGETABLES

My garden... was precisely the right extent. An hour or two of morning labour was all that it required. But I used to visit and revisit it a dozen times a day, and stand in deep contemplation over my vegetable progeny, with a love that nobody could share or conceive of, who had never taken part in the process of creation. It was one of the most bewitching sights in the world to observe a hill of beans thrusting through the soil, or a row of early peas just peeping forth sufficiently to trace a line of delicate green.

-Nathaniel Hawthorne

ADMIRATION FOR A GARDENER PLANTING POTATOES

The way in which he was planting potatoes was wonderful, every potato was placed at exactly the right distance apart, and a hole made for it in the general trench; before it was set it was looked at and turned over, and the thumb rubbed against it to be sure that it was sound, and when finally put in, a little mould was delicately adjusted round to keep it in its right position till the whole row was buried. He carried the potatoes in his coat pocket - those, that is, for the row - and took them out one by one; had he been planting his own children he could not have been more careful. The science, the skill, and the experience brought to this potato planting you would hardly credit; for all this care was founded upon observation, and arose from very large abilities on the part of the planter, though directed to so humble a purpose at that moment.

-Richard Jeffries,
Amaryllis at the Fair

I want death to find me planting my cabbages.
                                        -Montaigne

18

19

20

1962-At the A.G.M. of the Horticultural Trades Association, Mr. Bygrave reported on the American innovation of growing plants in containers - specifically tin cans. The idea was taken up by British garden centres and the container plant revolution had begun.

21

22

23

24

THE BEST TYPE OF STATUE

Statues are also admissible in garden scenery, and should be large, as they are most effective when viewed at a distance; consequently, the outline of their form should be bold, the drapery rough and the figure so commanding as to assume its proper proportions at a distance of from 50 to 100 yards from the spectator. The best materials are stone, bronze, iron and lead, the last two named materials being painted to resemble stone. They are sometimes very effective in alcoves, summerhouses etc., and sometimes impart the charm of sudden surprise as suitable terminals to winding paths.

-The Beeton Book of
Garden Management

STATUES IN THE GARDEN

Getting it Wrong:

"Statues of marble seldom look well in Italy, never in England, and of all discords none can be so jarring as to place among the flowers dreadful forms of disease and suffering, cripples or beggars... Art, like laughter, should be the language of happiness, and those who suffer should be silent."

-George Sitwell

...And Getting it Right:

"Ensnared with the peace and the delightful seclusion we wander down an umbrageous grass glade. The springy turf under our feet, the sunshine, the birds, all join in the transcendent harmony of the soul and lead it to a region where, peering out from under a leaf canopy, we discern a statue of Pan with his reed pipes. The spell is complete."

-Thomas Mawson

THE ROLE OF THE CONSERVATORY FOR PLANTS AND PLEASURE

Conservatories first appeared on the British scene in the 17th century, when the word seems to have been used to mean a glass, or partly glass, structure in which plants and flowers could be protected from the elements and thus flourish, even throughout the winter. However, by the Victorian era the conservatory became clearly identified as different from a greenhouse, both in design and - to some extent - in purpose.

The Victorians developed the conservatory as an extension to the home, including relatively modest middle-class villas as well as great houses. The most ambitious and renowned conservatories of the period were designed by Sir Joseph Paxton, gardener to the Duke of Devonshire at Chatsworth and a talented architect. The Great Conservatory at Chatsworth was a huge structure that took four years to build and generated great excitement. Paxton then went on to design the Crystal Palace, which was erected in Hyde Park in 1851 for the Great Exhibition.

England - a happy land we know,
Where follies naturally grow.
                    -Charles Churchill

25

1878-Awards announced at the Paris Exhibition, horticultural section.

26

27

28

29

30

31

The Style and Elegance of a Bygone Era

Priory Conservatories have been designing and building the finest Hardwood and Redwood tailor-made conservatories for the past 10 years.

Prior to that much of the specialist carpentry work undertaken was in the field of restoration and refurbishment of old Victorian Conservatories.

In recent years however, Victorian style conservatories have been steadily increasing in popularity, so much so that they are now becoming quite a common sight, and not just for the rich and famous as they were in the Victorian and Edwardian eras.

A characteristic of the Victorians was their ingenuity, the attention to detail, and their ability to design a building that complements and is complemented by its surroundings. These are traditional values that we adhere to at Priory. Designing a conservatory goes far beyond creating modular sections in pre-frabricated units; every property is different and should be treated as such. Having a conservatory added to your home as a permanent extension should be seen as an asset, so make sure you are not disappointed. Call in:- *The Conservatory Professionals - Priory Conservatories.*

The delightful rural setting, an old country cottage and a Priory Conservatory. (Designed, Manufactured, Built and Illustrated for a client, 1989)

Priory Conservatories

The Conservatory Professionals

A Traditional Victorian Style Conservatory

For the finest Conservatories & Summerhouses money can buy, designed and manufactured exclusively to your requirements, you need look no further than Priory who can offer you the following:-

- Attention to detail and customer service that is second to none.
- Specialists in Conservatories for listed buildings.
- Total project undertaken from design to completion by OUR OWN craftsmen (No sub-contractors).
- Quotes, surveys and colour drawings FREE of charge and with NO-OBLIGATION, undertaken personally by a director of the Company.
- Traditional old fashioned service.
- Comprehensive Guarantee.
- No salesmen.
- Designs, limited only by imagination, that blend in with their surroundings perfectly.
- A Company director who oversees every stage of a project however large or small.

Priory Conservatories are exhibitors at most of the major horticultural shows in the U.K. calendar, including The Chelsea Flower Show and The Hampton Court International Flower Show

An Elegant Modern Conservatory in English Oak

For our colour brochure, more information or to arrange a free survey, write or telephone:

Fosmop House, 50 Albert Road North, Reigate, Surrey RH2 9EL

(0737) 221296 or 222783. Fax (0737) 224961

In the other gardens
And all up the vale,
From the autumn bonfires
See the smoke trails!

Pleasant summer over
And all the summer flowers,
The red fire blazes,
The grey smoke towers.

-Robert Louis Stevenson

BURNING OF AN OAK 1,100 YEARS OLD, 1892

Early on Saturday an unusual spectacle was witnessed in the Home Park at Hampton Court, when a magnificent Oak, growing about 200 yards from the Long Water, was discovered to be on fire. It is said to be 1,100 years old and one of the largest Oaks in England. It is 33ft. in circumference having an average diameter of 11 feet. The trunk was hollow for about 10ft., and several of the larger branches above that are also in a decayed condition. The fire was extinguished in a few hours, but not before the tree had been almost consumed. The cause of the fire is unknown.

-Gardeners Chronicle

A LETTER FROM THE THIRD EARL OF PEMBROKE TO THE SHERIFF OF STAFFORDSHIRE

Sir-

His majesty, taking notice that the burning of Ferne doth draw down raine, and being desirous that the country and himself may enjoy fair weather as long as he remains in these parts, His Majesty has commanded me to write to you to cause all burning of Ferne to be forborne until His Majesty be past the country.

Your very loving friend,
Pembroke and Montgomery

THE ART OF THE BONFIRE

A bonfire will burn for days and consume all sorts of rubbish. It should be started with paper and a few dry sticks; damp material must not be put on until the fire is burning well. The centre of the heap of rubbish must be kept loose to allow a draught of air to penetrate. When the fire is burning freely, damp rubbish should be placed around the outside so that it will dry somewhat and thus burn more readily when placed on the fire.

The best time to light a bonfire is in dry weather when there is some wind. If the garden is surrounded by other gardens a day should be chosen, if possible, when the wind is in such a direction as that it will carry the smoke away from the neighbours.

The ash, called wood-ash, the residue of the bonfire, should be collected and stored under cover, for it is a valuable potash fertiliser for use in the flower, fruit and kitchen garden. If left exposed to the rain, however, the potash is soon lost.

THE FALLING OF THE LEAVES

Autumn is over the long leaves that love us,
And over the mice in the barley sheaves;
Yellow the leaves of the rowan above us,
And yellow the wet wild-strawberry leaves.

-W.B. Yeats

1

1865-Joseph Hooker appointed Director of the Royal Botanic Gardens, Kew in succession to his father, Sir William Hooker, who had become the first Director of Kew in 1841.

2

1993-Flower Show at the R.H.S. Halls, Westminster featuring ornamental plants and botanical paintings.

3

4

5

1993-National Chrysanthemum Society Show, R.H.S. New Hall, Westminster.

6

7

THE APPEAL OF ROCKERIES

These ornaments of the garden, although not absolutely necessary are, nevertheless, pleasing objects of importance in a good-finished pleasure-ground, but indispensable to those gardens where a class of plants can only be at home upon them, and which it is desired to grow.

A rockery displays itself to the best advantage when it is backed by evergreen trees and shrubs, and overhung with laburnum and willow. These not only afford an agreeable accessory to a good piece of rockery, but a most desirable shade for the plants growing upon it.

A bit of rockwork may be made to imitate a large stone rising out of a pool, but unless it is of a different class from one of the inland kind, and furnished accordingly, it is out of place. If rock-constructors would gain a knowledge of natural rockeries, they would find it not so difficult to accomplish their object; this is easily done nowadays. Photography is a boon in this respect; facsimiles of rockeries can now be had for a trifle, which will be good for guides in forming new ones.

-Samuel Wood, *Good Gardening*, 1876

EXPERT ADVICE ON CREATING A NATURAL ROCK GARDEN

The whole aim and object of a natural rock garden is to create a picture of interest and beauty, irrespective of labour - to have a spot somewhere to which we can always go for rest and peace; just one place where, even in winter, we do not have dead flowers only to contemplate, or bare earth awaiting the bedding out. Some corner where, out of the flowering season, beauty of line will satisfy.

...Proportion, balance, simplicity are the keynotes; restraint the tune. Success lies not in owning a thousand tons of rock nor every kind of plant, nor boasting many gardeners. It lies in the feeling of rest that the whole finished work can give.

-B.H.B. Symons-Jeune, *Natural Rock Gardening*, 1932

STINGING CRITICISM OF ROCK GARDENERS FROM REGINALD FARRER, 1914

It is in the rock-garden that we show at once our best and worse. Our love of the craft, and our skill in it, have grown to something quite amazing. But we have not yet fully developed both the horticultural and the architectural elements of the rock-garden. We are still, in fact, too blind or indifferent to the existence of an architectural element in the rock-garden at all... We still think that any odd corner is good enough to bear the name... Most unbearable of all things is the too common rock-garden, chucked together blindly, as if any chaos were sufficient, or built of fried cement, or some artificial concoction baked into stalactites. Why do so many people think that the rock-garden is the happy home of anarchy and unguided personal whim? Why do so many people seem to think that rule and composition are here of no importance, or non-existent - *here*, where they are if possible, far more vital than in more formal circumstances? For the laws of plain gardening are evident: the right rhythm of wildness is harder and more subtle to catch.

Nature always works with slowness, and, so to speak, with thriftness.

-Montesquieu

8

9

10

1892-First annual exhibition of the Windsor, Eton and District Chrysanthemum and Horticultural Society.

11

12

13

14

THE ELDER - A CURE FOR ALL ILLS

If the medicinal properties of the leaves, bark, berries etc. were thoroughly known, I cannot tell what our countrymen could ail, for which he might not fetch a remedy from every hedge, either for sickness or wound.

-John Evelyn

GROWING AND SMOKING TOBACCO

I have committed some to the earth in the end of March, some in April, and some in the beginning of May, because I durst not hazard all my seed at one time... The dry leaves are used to be taken in a pipe set on fire and suckt into the stomacke against the pains in the head, rheumes, aches in any part of the bodie... Those leaves do palliate or ease for a time but never perform any cure absolutely. Some use to smoke it for wantoness, or rather custom; which kind of taking is unwholesome and very dangerous.

-Gerard

ESSENTIAL HERBS TO GROW IN THE PHYSIC GARDEN

Annis; Archangel; Betanie; Chervil; Cinqfile; Detanie or garden ginger; Dragons; Gromsel seed for the stone; Hartstrong; Horehound; Lovage for the stone; Licoras; Mandrake; Mugwort; Pionees; Poppie; Rue; Rhubarb; Savin for the bots; Smalach for swellings; Stitchwort; Valerian; Woodbine.

Thus ends in breefe

Of herbes the chief

To get more skill

Read whom ye will

Such mo to have

Of field go crave

-Thomas Tusser, 1573

SAGE - A FERTILITY DRUG

Sage causeth women to be fertile, wherefore in times past the people of Egypt, after a great mortality and plague, constrained their women to drink the juice thereof, to cause them the sooner to conceive and bring forth store of children.

-Henry Lyte

THE VERY USEFUL THISTLE

It sharpeneth the wit and memorie, strengthneth all the principall parts of the bodie, quickneth all the sense, comforteth the stomacke, procureth appetite, and hath a special vertue against poyson, and preserveth from the Pestilence, and is excellent good against any kinde of Fever.

-Cogan, Haven of Health

COMMON RED POPPY.

GREATER CELANDINE. CHELIDONIUM MAJUS.

PAPAVER RHOEAS.

YELLOW HORNED POPPY. GLAUCIUM FLAVUM.

COMMON WELSH POPPY. MECONOPSIS CAMBRICA.

His Aunt Jobiska made him drink
Lavender water tinged with pink,
For she said, "The world in general knows
There's nothing so good for a Pobble's toes!"
-Edward Lear, *The Pobble who has no toes*

15

1719-Death of John Parkinson, author of *Paradisi in Solo, Paradisus Terrestris*.

16

17

18

19

20

21

Small birds - to scare from seeds: stick a few potatoes all over with white feathers, and suspend them a few inches from the ground, by means of a few threads of red worsted passed across your seed beds.

-William Jones, The Gardener's Receipt Book, 1858

SWAP-HOOKS AND SICKLES

The swap-hook or sickle, has more agricultural than garden importance. But Henderson, in 1888, writes that it is "a most useful implement for switching around and trimming off grass under hedges, bushes, fences". Of the scythe he writes "The lawn scythe is now but little used, the lawn-mower taking its place, unless on hill-sides or among tress or shrubs, where the lawn-mower cannot be worked."

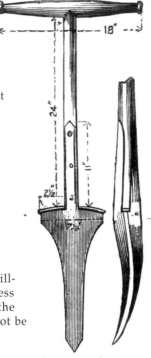

MUNRO'S PERFORATOR

THE WATERING CAN

Plants have always needed water, and young, tender plants have needed the water to be sprinkled on them with care. Around 800 A.D., the monk Walafrid Strabo tells how he used his fingers to spread the flow of water from his bucket, so that it fell *guttatim* or "drop by drop" on to his seedlings. The watering-pot made of earthenware, was invented in the late Middle Ages, though buckets and jars were - and are still -used. In 1577, Tusser writes of "watering with pot or with dish."

HOES AND RAKES

Rakes are always pulled towards the gardener as are some hoes - *draw*-hoes. Philip Miller's *Gardener's Dictionary* gives three sizes - the *onion* hoe, the smallest, was no more than 3" wide; the *carrot* hoe, 4.5" and the *turnip* hoe, 7.5". Other hoes - *thrust*- or *push*-hoes - are pushed away. These include the Scuffle or Dutch hoe and the Spud. Cobbett was emphatic that the hoe with prongs tines or *spanes* (rather like the "fork cultivator") was the best implement. "A mere *flat*-hoeing does nothing but keep down the weeds. The hoeing when the plants are becoming stout, should be deep; and, in general, with a hoe that has *spanes*, instead of a mere flat plate. In short a sort of *prong* in the *posture* of a hoe... "

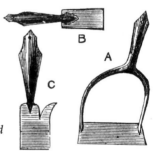

VARIETIES OF THE THRUST HOE

A. *Scuffle or Dutch Hoe*

B. *Spud.*

C. *Combined Spud and Weed Hook.*

DIBBLES OR DIBBERS

The "debbyll, or setting stycke" comes in varied sizes, but its purpose is constant - to make a hole or depression in the soil, into which a seedling, cutting, large seed or bulb may be set - as in Shakespeare's 'I'll not put... The Dibble in earth, to set on slip of them'

-(*Winter's Tale*, IV.iv.100)

The dibble or dibber... an indispensable tool... for the transference of most plants that are grown in seed beds... and then planted apart at wider intervals.

-Beeton, Garden Management, c.1890

Despite all the attractions of the world of publicity and entertainment my heart still stayed - and always will stay - in the garden and among the plants I love.

-Percy Thrower

22

23

24

25

1871-First publication of *The Garden* magazine by William Robinson, at a cover price of fourpence per week. The magazine became the main source of gardening information and Robinson edited it for 29 years.

26

27

28

VISIT YOUR NEAREST
NOTCUTTS GARDEN CENTRE

● Stratford Road,
Shirley, Solihull
WEST MIDLANDS
(021 744) 4501

● Oundle Road,
Orton Waterville,
PETERBOROUGH
(0733) 234600

Daniels Road,
NORWICH ●
(0603) 53155

Ipswich Road,
WOODBRIDGE ●
(0394) 383344

● Mattocks Rose Nurseries,
Nuneham Courtenay,
OXFORD.
(086 738) 454

● Hatfield Road,
Smallford,
ST ALBANS.
(0727) 53224

Station Road,
Ardleigh, ●
COLCHESTER
(0206) 230271

● Waterers Nurseries,
London Road,
BAGSHOT.
(0276) 472288

● Newnham Court,
Bearsted Road,
MAIDSTONE.
(0622) 39944

Tonbridge Road,
Pembury, ●
TUNBRIDGE WELLS.
(0892) 822636

● Guildford Road,
CRANLEIGH.
(0483) 274222

A GRAPHIC EXPLANATION OF FARMYARD MANURE

Dean Hole was a great rose grower, who always fed his roses liberally in November with farmyard manure, by which he meant: **"All the manures of the straw yard, solid and fluid, horse, cow, pig, poultry, in conjunction. Let a heap be made near the Rosarium, not suppressing the fumes of a natural fermentation by an external covering, but forming underneath a central drain, having lateral feeders, and at the lower end an external tank, after the fashion of those huge dinner dishes whose channels carry to the 'well', the dark gravies of the baron and the haunch (here that fastidious reader collapses, and is removed in a state of syncope), so that the rich extract, full of carbonate of ammonia, and precious as attar, may not be wasted, but may be used either as a liquid manure in the Rosary, or pumped back again to baste the beef."**

THE BEST SOURCES OF MANURE
(in order of effectiveness) - 1725

1. Bird Dung, especially that of Pigeons and Doves (A small quantity of it sprinkled on ground enriches it extremely).

2. The Dung of men mixed with soil taken out of the streets (It is of a very hot nature of itself and should not be used alone).

3. Man's urine lain to mellow and digest for six months before use (There is nothing which contributes more to the welfare of vines and fruit trees).

4. The Dung of Cattle - the best is that of Asses (These creatures eat very slowly and have a quick digestion).

DISTINGUISHED BY A HUMBLE SPARROW

I once had a sparrow alight on my shoulder for a moment while I was hoeing in a village garden and I felt that I was more distinguished by that circumstance than I should have been by any epaulet I could have worn.

-H.D. Thoreau

BLACKBIRDS AND THRUSHES OBSERVED

Blackbirds and Thrushes particularly the former feed in hard winters upon the shell snail horns by hunting them from the hedge bottoms and wood stumps and taking them to a stone where they break them in a very dexterous manner. Any curious observer of nature... will quickly see one of these birds... he then extracts the snail and like a true sportsman eagerly hastens to hunt them again in the hedges or woods where a frequent rustle of their little feet is heard among the dead leaves.

-John Clare

*A*t the corner of Wood Street, when daylight appears,
Hangs a Thrush that sings loud, it has sung for three years;
Poor Susan has passed by the spot, and has heard
In the silence of morning the song of the Bird.

'Tis a note of enchantment; what ails her? She sees
A mountain ascending, a vision of trees;
Bright volumes of vapour through Lothbury glide,
And a river flows on through the vale of Cheapside.

-Wordsworth, The Reverie of
Poor Susan

With the near approach of the Peace Settlement the paper problem becomes less acute, and we are now in a position to accept more advertisements than hitherto.

-Gardeners Chronicle, 1919

29

1843-Birth of Gertrude Jekyll, Piccadilly, London.

30

1

2

3

4

5

1926-Death of Claude Monet at Giverny, the garden that he created and painted many times.

SOME COMMON BRITISH GARDEN BIRDS

Blackbird
Feeds on insects and larvae, earthworms, fruit and seeds

Robin
Feeds on insects and larvae in spring and summer, seeds in winter

House Sparrow
Feeds on grain and weed seeds, insects, bread and food scraps

Blue Tit
Feeds on aphids, caterpillars, fruit, grain and seeds

Great Tit
Feeds on insects, aphids, buds, fruit, seeds, peas

Song Thrush
Feeds on snails, earthworms, insects, seeds and fruit

Mistle Thrush
Feeds on fruit and berries, insects, snails, earthworms

Collared Dove
Feeds on grain and weed seeds and fruit

Wren
Feeds on insects and larvae, spiders and seeds

Chaffinch
Feeds on seeds, beech-mast, grain

Greenfinch
Feeds on seeds, berries and wild fruit

Bullfinch
Feeds on seeds, weeds, berries, caterpillars, fruit tree buds

Goldfinch
Feeds on weed seeds, tree fruit and insects

AT DAY-CLOSE IN NOVEMBER

The ten hours' light is abating,
And a late bird wings across.
Where the pines, like waltzers waiting,
Give their black heads a toss.

Beech leaves that yellow the noontime,
Float past like specks in the eye;
I set every tree in my June time,
And now they obscure the sky.

And the children who ramble through here
Conceive that there never has been
A time when no tall trees grew here,
That none will in time be seen.

-Thomas Hardy

I value my garden more for being full of blackbirds than of cherries, and very frankly give them fruit for their songs.

-Addison

DECEMBER

6

1908-Sale of 2,468 cases of Japanese Lilies was held at 67 & 68 Cheapside, London.

7

8

9

10

11

12

EARLY DAYS OF A GREAT PLANTSMAN:
Roy Lancaster on his career...

When I left school at the age of fifteen I joined the local Bolton Parks Department. This I admit was my second choice to becoming an engine driver because steam locomotives excited me as much as plants. For two happy years I worked at Moss Bank Park and it was here that my interest in plants really began to take root.

...AND AN UNNERVING INCIDENT WITH A ROOT

Once, I was working in a cemetery near Bolton when many of the gravediggers had gone down with colds or flu. Because of the pressure, I was drafted in to help throw back soil excavated by one of the few diggers still on duty. When he had dug to a depth of 6 feet he exclaimed, "Hey, look at this!" I peered in to the grave, fearing what I might find, but was relieved to see him holding only the long, black, thong-like root of common horsetail - because of the situation I have never forgotten this incident.

- In Search of
the Wild Asparagus

from cold winds, shade for woodland plants, a place for birds to nest and, in the long dull months of an English winter, a backcloth of continuous interest.

Twenty-five years ago there were few dwarf and slow growing garden conifers available. Since then the range of new forms has increased enormously, to meet demand, and now we are almost spoilt for choice.

ADRIAN BLOOM ON CONIFERS IN A DULL ENGLISH WINTER

Conifers provide an amazing range of forms and colours for year round interest, yet most require little maintenance.

Since I first became interested in conifers twenty-five years ago, I have come to appreciate their worth fully, especially in my own garden at Foggy Bottom. As it gradually developed from an open, wind-swept field, the taller conifers grew to provide shelter for other plants. These conifers now give respite

PLANNING FOR POSTERITY

I am a great believer in planning and planting for the future. When I have completed some development in the garden, or planted a new tree, I suggest to my friends that we should meet one hundred years hence, to the minute, to see the result. "You come down", I tell them, "and I'll get special permission to come up".

-Charles, Lord Aberconway

13

14

1843-Death of John Claudius Loudon, landscape gardener, architect and prolific writer of books and encyclopaedias. His wife, Jane, was also a famous writer, her best known book being *The Ladies' Companion to the Flower Garden.*

15

16

17

18

19

CHRISTMASS

Christmass is come and every hearth
Makes room to give him welcome now.
Een want will dry its tears in mirth
And crown him with a holly bough.
Tho tramping neath a winters sky
Oer snow track paths and rhymey stiles
The huswife sets her spinning bye
And buds him welcome with her smile.

The shepherd now no more afraid
Since custom doth the chance bestow
Starts up to kiss the giggling maid
Beneath the branch of mizzletoe
That neath each cottage beam is seen
Wi pearl-like berrys shining gay
The shadow still of what hath been
Which fashion yearly fades away.

-John Clare

CHRISTMAS TREES ARE PLANTS, TOO

The Christmas Tree, Picea Abies or the Common Spruce comes from the mountains of central Europe, where it ascends to an altitude of 6,000ft., to almost the limit of tree growth in northerly regions. At its best it may grow 150-200ft. high, with a girth of 15-20ft., although the average is less, and in the more exposed and northerly regions it dwindles to a bush. It is very

variable in habit, in having hairy or hairless shoots, and in the length of the leaves. The leaves usually persist for several years and the pendulous cones are cylindrical and 4-6 in. long. The seeds ripen in autumn.

-The Popular Encyclopaedia
of Gardening

MISTLETOE

The common Mistletoe, Viscum album, is an evergreen parasitic shrub that usually grows on Apple, Lime, Maple, Poplar, Willow or Hawthorn trees, although it is frequently associated with Oak trees. Folklore says that Mistletoe was once a fine tree with a stately trunk, but was cut down to use as the cross for Christ's crucifixion, and it was then ordained for ever more that it should depend on another tree for its existence.

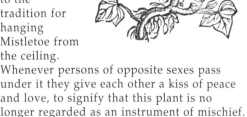

Scandinavian mythology led to the tradition for hanging Mistletoe from the ceiling. Whenever persons of opposite sexes pass under it they give each other a kiss of peace and love, to signify that this plant is no longer regarded as an instrument of mischief.

T he mystic Mistltoe,
Which has no root and cannot grow
Or prosper but by that same tree
It clings to.

-Ancient Welsh verse

A Robin Redbreast in a cage
Puts all heaven in a rage.
-William Blake

DECEMBER

20

21

1864-Probably on this day, Edwin Hillier bought a nurseryman and florist's business in Winchester, which grew to become the famous nursery business of Hillier and Sons.

22

23

24

25

26

FOR GARDENERS WHO HAD TO DO THEIR OWN WEATHER FORECASTING

Keep a book, with each page divided into columns. Note the day of the month and week, and at fixed times each day record the following items:

1. How the quicksilver rises or falls in the Barometer.

2. What is the alteration of the Hygrometer.

3. How the spirits in the Thermometer rise or fall.

4. From what point of the Compass the wind blows and the strength of the wind, according to the nearest guess.

5. Whether it rains, snows, hails etcetera.

After some time, patterns will emerge and it will be possible to predict the forthcoming weather from patterns that have gone before.

TABLE OF MEASURES OF CAPACITY

- ❏ 1 gallon = 277 cubic inches
- ❏ 6³/₄ gallons = 1 cubic foot
- ❏ 1 bushel = 2,220 cubic inches
- ❏ 8 gallons = 1 bushel
- ❏ 21 bushels = 1 cubic yard

SNOW STORM

What a night the wind howls and hisses and but stops
To howl more loud while the snow volley keeps
Incessant batter at the window pane
Making our comfort feel as sweet again
And in the morning when the tempest drops
At every cottage door mountainous heaps
Of snow lies drifted that all the entrance stops
Until the besom and the shovel gains
The Path - and leaves a wall on either side -
The shepherd rambling valleys white and wide
With new sensations his old memorys fills
When hedges left at night no more descried
Are turned to one white sweep of curving hills
And trees turned bushes half their bodies hide

-John Clare

Blow, blow, thou winter wind,
Thou art not so unkind
As man's ingratitude:
Thy tooth is not so keen,
Because thou art not seen,
Although thy breath be rude.
Heigh-ho! sing, heigh-ho! unto the green holly:
Most friendship is feigning, most loving mere folly.
Then heigh-ho! the holly!
This life is most jolly.

-William Shakespeare

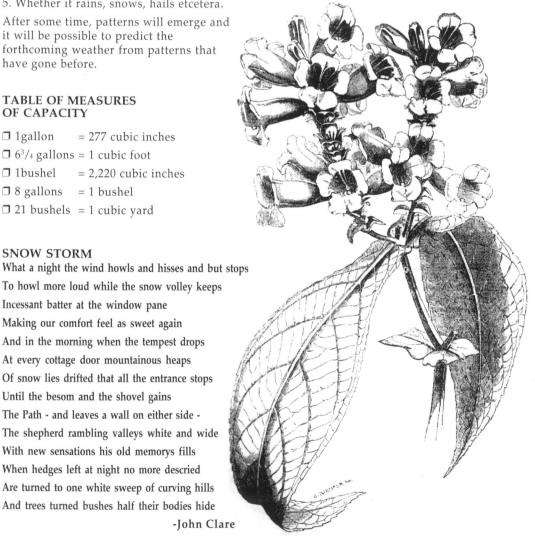

The summer never shines so bright
As thought of in a winter's night.
-Thomas Hood

27

28

29

30

31

1

2

1993

January

S	M	T	W	T	F	S
					1	2
3	4	5	6	7	8	9
10	11	12	13	14	15	16
17	18	19	20	21	22	23
24	25	26	27	28	29	30
31						

February

S	M	T	W	T	F	S
	1	2	3	4	5	6
7	8	9	10	11	12	13
14	15	16	17	18	19	20
21	22	23	24	25	26	27
28						

March

S	M	T	W	T	F	S
	1	2	3	4	5	6
7	8	9	10	11	12	13
14	15	16	17	18	19	20
21	22	23	24	25	26	27
28	29	30	31			

April

S	M	T	W	T	F	S
				1	2	3
4	5	6	7	8	9	10
11	12	13	14	15	16	17
18	19	20	21	22	23	24
25	26	27	28	29	30	

May

S	M	T	W	T	F	S
						1
2	3	4	5	6	7	8
9	10	11	12	13	14	15
16	17	18	19	20	21	22
23	24	25	26	27	28	29
30	31					

June

S	M	T	W	T	F	S
		1	2	3	4	5
6	7	8	9	10	11	12
13	14	15	16	17	18	19
20	21	22	23	24	25	26
27	28	29	30			

July

S	M	T	W	T	F	S
				1	2	3
4	5	6	7	8	9	10
11	12	13	14	15	16	17
18	19	20	21	22	23	24
25	26	27	28	29	30	31

August

S	M	T	W	T	F	S
1	2	3	4	5	6	7
8	9	10	11	12	13	14
15	16	17	18	19	20	21
22	23	24	25	26	27	28
29	30	31				

September

S	M	T	W	T	F	S
			1	2	3	4
5	6	7	8	9	10	11
12	13	14	15	16	17	18
19	20	21	22	23	24	25
26	27	28	29	30		

October

S	M	T	W	T	F	S
					1	2
3	4	5	6	7	8	9
10	11	12	13	14	15	16
17	18	19	20	21	22	23
24	25	26	27	28	29	30
31						

November

S	M	T	W	T	F	S
	1	2	3	4	5	6
7	8	9	10	11	12	13
14	15	16	17	18	19	20
21	22	23	24	25	26	27
28	29	30				

December

S	M	T	W	T	F	S
			1	2	3	4
5	6	7	8	9	10	11
12	13	14	15	16	17	18
19	20	21	22	23	24	25
26	27	28	29	30	31	

1992

January
S	M	T	W	T	F	S
			1	2	3	4
5	6	7	8	9	10	11
12	13	14	15	16	17	18
19	20	21	22	23	24	25
26	27	28	29	30	31	

February
S	M	T	W	T	F	S
						1
2	3	4	5	6	7	8
9	10	11	12	13	14	15
16	17	18	19	20	21	22
23	24	25	26	27	28	29

March
S	M	T	W	T	F	S
1	2	3	4	5	6	7
8	9	10	11	12	13	14
15	16	17	18	19	20	21
22	23	24	25	26	27	28
29	30	31				

April
S	M	T	W	T	F	S
			1	2	3	4
5	6	7	8	9	10	11
12	13	14	15	16	17	18
19	20	21	22	23	24	25
26	27	28	29	30		

May
S	M	T	W	T	F	S
					1	2
3	4	5	6	7	8	9
10	11	12	13	14	15	16
17	18	19	20	21	22	23
24	25	26	27	28	29	30
31						

June
S	M	T	W	T	F	S
	1	2	3	4	5	6
7	8	9	10	11	12	13
14	15	16	17	18	19	20
21	22	23	24	25	26	27
28	29	30				

July
S	M	T	W	T	F	S
			1	2	3	4
5	6	7	8	9	10	11
12	13	14	15	16	17	18
19	20	21	22	23	24	25
26	27	28	29	30	31	

August
S	M	T	W	T	F	S
						1
2	3	4	5	6	7	8
9	10	11	12	13	14	15
16	17	18	19	20	21	22
23	24	25	26	27	28	29
30	31					

September
S	M	T	W	T	F	S
		1	2	3	4	5
6	7	8	9	10	11	12
13	14	15	16	17	18	19
20	21	22	23	24	25	26
27	28	29	30			

October
S	M	T	W	T	F	S
				1	2	3
4	5	6	7	8	9	10
11	12	13	14	15	16	17
18	19	20	21	22	23	24
25	26	27	28	29	30	31

November
S	M	T	W	T	F	S
1	2	3	4	5	6	7
8	9	10	11	12	13	14
15	16	17	18	19	20	21
22	23	24	25	26	27	28
29	30					

December
S	M	T	W	T	F	S
		1	2	3	4	5
6	7	8	9	10	11	12
13	14	15	16	17	18	19
20	21	22	23	24	25	26
27	28	29	30	31		

1994

January
S	M	T	W	T	F	S
						1
2	3	4	5	6	7	8
9	10	11	12	13	14	15
16	17	18	19	20	21	22
23	24	25	26	27	28	29
30	31					

February
S	M	T	W	T	F	S
		1	2	3	4	5
6	7	8	9	10	11	12
13	14	15	16	17	18	19
20	21	22	23	24	25	26
27	28					

March
S	M	T	W	T	F	S
		1	2	3	4	5
6	7	8	9	10	11	12
13	14	15	16	17	18	19
20	21	22	23	24	25	26
27	28	29	30	31		

April
S	M	T	W	T	F	S
					1	2
3	4	5	6	7	8	9
10	11	12	13	14	15	16
17	18	19	20	21	22	23
24	25	26	27	28	29	30

May
S	M	T	W	T	F	S
1	2	3	4	5	6	7
8	9	10	11	12	13	14
15	16	17	18	19	20	21
22	23	24	25	26	27	28
29	30	31				

June
S	M	T	W	T	F	S
			1	2	3	4
5	6	7	8	9	10	11
12	13	14	15	16	17	18
19	20	21	22	23	24	25
26	27	28	29	30		

July
S	M	T	W	T	F	S
					1	2
3	4	5	6	7	8	9
10	11	12	13	14	15	16
17	18	19	20	21	22	23
24	25	26	27	28	29	30
31						

August
S	M	T	W	T	F	S
	1	2	3	4	5	6
7	8	9	10	11	12	13
14	15	16	17	18	19	20
21	22	23	24	25	26	27
28	29	30	31			

September
S	M	T	W	T	F	S
				1	2	3
4	5	6	7	8	9	10
11	12	13	14	15	16	17
18	19	20	21	22	23	24
25	26	27	28	29	30	

October
S	M	T	W	T	F	S
						1
2	3	4	5	6	7	8
9	10	11	12	13	14	15
16	17	18	19	20	21	22
23	24	25	26	27	28	29
30	31					

November
S	M	T	W	T	F	S
		1	2	3	4	5
6	7	8	9	10	11	12
13	14	15	16	17	18	19
20	21	22	23	24	25	26
27	28	29	30			

December
S	M	T	W	T	F	S
				1	2	3
4	5	6	7	8	9	10
11	12	13	14	15	16	17
18	19	20	21	22	23	24
25	26	27	28	29	30	31

INDEX

A

Aberconway, Lord, Charles   126
Allotments   84
Arnold, Matthew   64

B

Bacon, Francis   70
Banks, Sir Joseph   38
Baskets
   hanging   72
   suspended   72
Bees   64, 74, 104
   first flight of   102
   uniting of   102
Birds
   Blackbirds   122
   common types of   124
   Sparrow   122
   Thrushes   122
Blomfield, Reginald   48
Boilers   52, 104
Bonfires
   art of   112
Borders
   herbaceous   42
Budding, Edward, Beard   36
Butterflies   80

C

Carroll, Lewis   76
Celandine   30
Chelsea Flower Show   52
Christmas   128
Clare, John   30, 128, 130
Cobbett, William   100
Conservatories   108
Cottages   6, 48, 60, 64, 70, 128, 130
Covent Garden   6, 90

D

Digging
   in praise of   12
   trenching   12

E

Earthworms
   facts about   80
Earwigs
   efficient trap for   72
Elder, the   116
Evelyn, John   116

F

Farrer, Reginald   8, 40, 114
Fencing
   arch   100
   creative   44

pergola   100
   rustic   100
   wattle hurdles   72
Flower beds   44
Flowers   22
   admonition for lovers of   54
   bell-shaped   64
Forsyth, William   38
Fountains
   interesting types   50
Fragrance
   cottage flowers   70
   Laced Pinks   70
   night-scented   70
   sweetly scented   670
Fruit trees,
  protection of   30
Fumigation   104
Fungicide
   Burgundy Mixture   68
   Bordeaux Mixture 68

G

Gardeners   6
   education of   90
Gardener's Chronicle, The   38, 112
Gardener's Receipt Book, The   118
Gardens
   amusing   40
   childhood   90
   cottage flower   48
   design   4
   English cottage   48
   Japanese   4
   pleasure of   6
   siting   4
   Sunday supplement   76
   thoughts in a   64
   wild   40
Gent, J.W.   50
Gentian   64, 94
Gerard   30, 54, 60, 82, 116
Gilpin, William   44
Good Gardening   114
Greenhouses
   boilers   52, 104
   regulating   104
   types of   104

H

Ha Ha, the   40
Hall, The Rev. J. Bernard   90
Hampton Court Palace Garden   40
Hardy, Thomas   20
Hawthorne, Nathaniel   106
Herbs
   drying and storing   82
   essential to grow   116

ACKNOWLEDGEMENTS

Colour Illustrations:

Pages 10, 38, 52, 106: Photographs by Derek Goard, published in *The Chelsea Flower Show* by Faith and Geoff Whiten (Cassells)

Pages 28, 64, 74, 116, 124: From *Wild Flowers of the British Isles* by H. Isabel Adams.

Page 42: From *The Horticultural Record*, 1914. Photograph by Derek Goard.

Page 92: *Tulips*, from *The Ladies Flower Garden of Ornamental Bulbous Plants*, Jane Loudon, 1841.

Text:

Page 26: *Propagation of Trees, Shrubs and Conifers* by Wilfred G. Sheat, (Macmillan), 1957

Page 80: *The Natural History of the Garden* by Michael Chinery (Collins).

Page 42: "A Practical Approach to the Flower Garden" by H.E. Bates, from the book *A Love of Flowers* by kind permission of the Estate of H.E. Bates.

Page 90: *Sido* by Colette, translated by Enid McLeod; extract by kind permission of Martin Secker Warburg Ltd., publisher.

Page 126: "Adrian Bloom on Conifers" from *Blooms of Bressingham Garden Plants* by Alan and Adrian Bloom (HarperCollins) by kind permission of Adrian Bloom; *In Search of Wild Asparagus* by Roy Lancaster (Unwin Hyman) by kind permission of Roy Lancaster.

The Publishers would like to express their thanks to all the companies that appear in this book for their sponsorship support.

Dedication

The Publishers have dedicated this book in memory of Eric Belton, gardener, 1920-1992

Notes for Gardeners

Notes for Gardeners

Notes for Gardeners

Notes for Gardeners